Bone in action

B-1 Lancer

By Lou Drendel

Color by Lou Drendel

Illustrated by Mariano Rosales and Richard Hudson

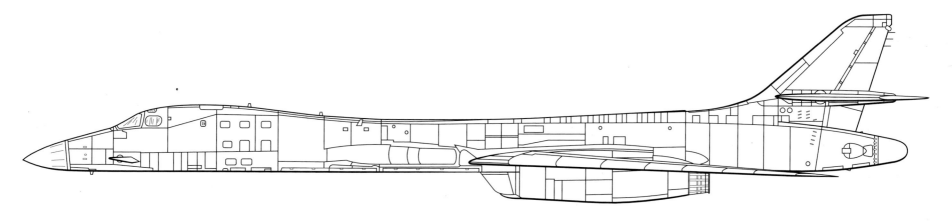

Aircraft Number 179

squadron/signal publications

A B-1B Lancer, named On Defense (85-0135), releases 500 pound (226.8 KG) Mk 82 retarded bombs over a bombing range in the southwestern United States. The bomber is assigned to the 28th Bomb Squadron (BS), 7th Bomb Wing (BW) at Dyess Air Force Base (AFB), Texas. This 'Bone' flew on both Operation DESERT FOX missions over Iraq – on 18 December and 19 December 1998 – while assigned to the 9th BS, 7th BW.

Foreword

Lt Col Davis 'Wally' Wallette is a big guy, built like a defensive lineman...an obvious choice as a prototypical B-52 pilot, strong enough to manhandle the huge 'BUFF' (Big Ugly Fat Fellow) around the sky, and quick enough to deal with its vagaries. Lt Col Wallette did fly the B-52 for a number of years before being assigned to the B-1B. 'Wally' was to be the leader of *Hawk* Flight, my B-1B sortie. His quick wit and command presence was evident during the briefing, and later, during a most eventful flight. That is why I feel duty bound to abide by his admonition to refrain from naming this book "B-1B Lancer In Action." Wally's exact quote was: *"Lou, whatever you do, DON'T call it 'Lancer In Action' "...it is a BONE. Everyone who flies it, maintains it, or refers to it in the Air Force, calls it 'BONE.'"*

That creates a little bit of a problem. To call the book "B-1 Bone In Action" is redundant, since BONE is a derivative of B-One. So, O.K. Wally, here it is..."BONE In Action." Thanks for the heads-up.

Photo Credits

Rockwell (now Boeing North American)
Lou Drendel
United States Air Force (USAF)
General Electric
John Gourley
Ted Carlson/Fotodynamics

Lt Col Tracy Sharp
Jeff Warmka
Scott Cameron
Frank Mirande
John Fietze
National Aeronautics and Space
   Administration (NASA)
Larry Davis

ISBN 0-89747-436-8

If you have any photographs of aircraft, armor, soldiers or ships of any nation, particularly wartime snapshots, why not share them with us and help make Squadron/Signal's books all the more interesting and complete in the future. Any photograph sent to us will be copied and the original returned. The donor will be fully credited for any photos used. Please send them to:

Squadron/Signal Publications, Inc.
1115 Crowley Drive
Carrollton, TX 75011-5010

Если у вас есть фотографии самолётов, вооружения, солдат или кораблей любой страны, особенно, снимки времён войны, поделитесь с нами и помогите сделать новые книги издательства Эскадрон/Сигнал ещё интереснее. Мы переснимем ваши фотографии и вернём оригиналы. Имена приславших снимки будут сопровождать все опубликованные фотографии. Пожалуйста, присылайте фотографии по адресу:

Squadron/Signal Publications, Inc.
1115 Crowley Drive
Carrollton, TX 75011-5010

軍用機、装甲車両、兵士、軍艦などの写真を所持しておられる方はいらっしゃいませんか？どの国のものでも結構です。作戦中に撮影されたものが特に良いのです。Squadron/Signal社の出版する刊行物において、このような写真は内容を一層充実し、興味深くすることができます。当方にお送り頂いた写真は、複写の後お返しいたします。出版物中に写真を使用した場合は、必ず提供者のお名前を明記させて頂きます。お写真は下記にご送付ください。

Squadron/Signal Publications, Inc.
1115 Crowley Drive
Carrollton, TX 75011-5010

The first B-1B Lancer (82-0001) flies in its element – high speed and low altitude – during a test flight from Rockwell's Palmdale, California assembly plant. Small fairings under the forward fuselage and engine nacelles house television cameras used for monitoring weapons separation. These fairings are not fitted to operational 'Bones.' Lancers were originally camouflaged in the 'Strategic Scheme' of Dark Gunship Gray (FS36081), Dark Green (FS34086), and Medium Gunship Gray (FS36118). (Rockwell)

Introduction

The Rockwell (Boeing North American since 1996) **B-1B Lancer**, popularly known as the 'Bone,' (a derivation of B-One), was a veteran of some of the toughest, life-threatening fighting long before it saw combat. Tracing its genesis to the 1960s, the B-1 began life as a United States Air Force (USAF) funded 1965 study for the Advanced Manned Strategic Aircraft (AMSA). AMSA was the follow-on program to the ill-fated North American **B-70 Valkyrie** triple-sonic high altitude strategic bomber.

The B-70 was planned to replace both the sub-sonic heavy lifting, but relatively slow Boeing **B-52 Stratofortress** and the double sonic, range and load-limited Convair **B-58 Hustler**. The USAF Air and Research Development Center (ARDC) issued weapons system requirements WS-110A and WS-125A in January of 1955. They respectively called for a conventional and a nuclear powered bomber capable of dash speeds of Mach 2 at high altitude, with a range of 1150 nautical miles (1324.2 statute miles/2131.1 KM). The Air Force wanted the bombers to be operational by 1963. Later in 1955, the USAF awarded preliminary study contracts to Boeing, North American, Douglas, Lockheed, Convair, and Martin. Convair and Lockheed were chosen to continue with the nuclear-powered bomber, while Boeing and North American worked on the conventionally powered aircraft.

The first attempts at meeting the conventional specification were submitted in October of 1956. Both were rejected as too large, complex, and expensive. Advances in engines and fuels resulted in new proposals by both contractors the following year. Weight was reduced by a third and range was extended to over 8000 miles (12,874.4 KM)! North American was selected as the winner of the conventional competition. 'Conventional' is really a misnomer, referring only to the relative conventionality – compared to a nuclear-powered aircraft – of what was now designated the XB-70. The contract for a single aircraft was awarded to North American on 31 December 1958. The nuclear-powered bomber proved to be too much of a technical challenge, and was shelved the same year.

The special fuels, which had promised increased range and power, were also too technically daunting and were deleted from the specifications. Fortunately, General Electric (GE) had developed a conventional engine that achieved 90% of the promised performance. The XB-70 was projected to have Mach 3 cruise speeds above 70,000 feet (21,336 M).

The late 1950s and early 1960s were notable for the ascendancy of rocketry. Intercontinental Ballistic Missiles (ICBMs) were proving to be more reliable and the promise of their devastating capabilities put bomber advocates on the defensive. ICBMs were advertised as being cheaper, more accurate, and faster than any bomber, current or projected. While they were ultimately not cheaper than the bombers, they were undeniably accurate and faster. They were also one-way, unequivocal, final solutions. Rockets in the form of Surface-to-Air Missiles (SAMs) were also used to deploy anti-aircraft defenses in the US and the Soviet Union. The Russians proved the ability of their defenses when, on 1 May 1960, they shot down a high-flying Lockheed **U-2** reconnaissance aircraft flown by Central Intelligence Agency (CIA) pilot Francis Gary Powers.

Although two XB-70 prototypes were built and flight-tested, the Valkyrie ultimately fell victim to the potentially fatal envelope of Russian SAMs and the absolutely fatal cost overruns associated with high profile leading edge technology development. While the SAMs did not prove to be a significant threat to triple sonic penetrators (no SAM ever shot down a Lockheed

The USAF's Advanced Manned Strategic Aircraft (AMSA) study, which spawned the B-1, sought a replacement for the Boeing B-52 Stratofortress. Instead, the Stratofortress would serve alongside Rockwell's new bomber. This B-52G (58-0184) was assigned to the 416th Bombardment Wing at Griffiss AFB, New York in 1986. (Frank Mirande)

The prototype Convair B-58A Hustler (55-660) flies over mountainous terrain during a test flight. The Hustler was the world's first supersonic bomber; however, its 5125 mile (8247.7 KM) unrefueled range and high operating cost shortened its service life. The B-58 served in the USAF between 1960 and 1970. (John Fietze)

SR-71 Blackbird), cost overruns were an almost indefensible target for the defense cutting tendencies of an increasingly anti-war and anti-military US Congress in the 1960s.

The manned bomber was far from dead, but the promise of a new bomber languished in a sea of quibbling while B-52s and ICBMs provided enough of a deterrent to Soviet expansionism throughout the 1960s. The Air Force wanted to make sure that their new bomber would include the latest offensive and defensive avionics and armaments, powered by the latest technology engine, including the most advanced aerodynamics and metallurgical components. This prompted endless studies of various concepts. The Subsonic Low Altitude Bomber (SLAB) transitioned to Extended Range Strike Aircraft (ERSA), morphed to Low Altitude Manned Penetrator (LAMP), then became Advanced Manned Precision Strike System (AMPSS), and finally the Advanced Manned Strategic Aircraft (AMSA). AMSA was the real beginning of the hoped-for successor to the B-52 fleet and a worthy standard bearer for the USAF image of global power projection, embodied by a long line of bombers.

The AMSA studies began in 1965 and concluded in 1969. They were subdivided into five major areas of operational concern. The propulsion study focused on the needed advanced technology engines. The alternate armament loading study examined the role of the AMSA as a conventional as well as nuclear bomber. The maintainability study sought ways to turn aircraft more quickly and to keep a maximum number of them flying. This was augmented by a reliability study. There was also a study concerning the use of titanium in structures. Titanium was relatively new at that time and the machining tools were extremely expensive. The four-year AMSA studies were exhaustive and detailed. They concluded with a Request For Proposals (RFP) on 3 November 1969.

Three major airframe and two engine manufacturers responded to the B-1 RFP. Boeing, General Dynamics (formerly Convair), and Rockwell (formerly North American) all had experience in the design of the B-52 follow-on, and they quickly presented their proposals. On 5 June 1970, Rockwell was awarded a contract for research, development, test, and evaluation of the prototype B-1. General Electric was chosen to develop the engines. The original contract called for five flying prototypes, two structural test airframes, and 40 engines. Delivery of the first of 244 B-1s to the USAF was scheduled for 1975, with the production run ending in 1981. This was modified in 1971 to three flying prototypes, one structural test airframe, and 27 engines.

The first XB-70A Valkyrie (62-0001) flies above a canyon in the southwestern United States in 1968. Both wingtips are folded down to improve high-speed stability and increase lift. After the XB-70 was cancelled as a bomber in 1964, the two prototypes were used for high-speed flight research. The second XB-70A was lost in a mid-air collision in 1966. NASA used 62-0001 for research flights until it was retired to the US Air Force Museum in 1969. (NASA)

Strategic Air Command (SAC) maintenance crews examine the B-1 mockup at Rockwell's Los Angeles, California facility in late 1971. The wooden mockup – open on the starboard side to show interior components – was examined by an Air Force review team. The team recommended 297 changes to the B-1's systems. Rockwell made these changes before completing the B-1 prototype in 1974. (Rockwell)

Development

B-1A Number One

B-1A Number Four (With 'Crosseye' ECM Spine)

B-1B Lancer

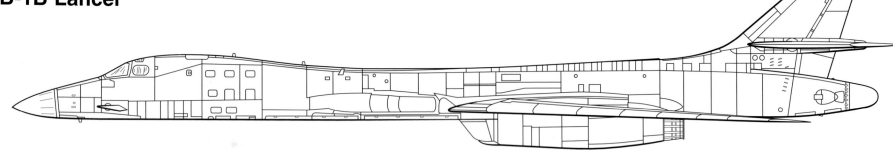

B-1A

Rockwell unveiled the **B-1A** full-scale mockup on 4 November 1971. A critical review of the mockup by Air Force officials resulted in 297 requests for changes. This was an indication of how complex the B-1 had become. Before the first aircraft flew, 22,000 hours of wind tunnel time had been expended to refine the airframe design. The B-1 employed a swing-wing design to enhance performance at either end of the operational envelope. The slim fuselage blended into long-chord wing roots, augmenting lift at all speeds. The variable geometry wing swept from 15°(fully extended) for low speed flight to 67.5° (fully swept aft) for high speed flight. They are equipped with full span slats, which can be extended 20° for takeoff and landing, and slatted flaps, which can be extended up to 40°. Flap extension is limited to sweep angles of 15 to 20°. Beyond 20°, hydraulic interlocks prevent operation of flaps and slats. The B-1 has no ailerons; roll is controlled by upper wing spoilers and by differential movement of the stabilators.

Long life was always a major consideration when designing the B-1. This led Rockwell to employ advanced fracture mechanics to select optimum metals for the airframe. Fracture mechanics enabled the Rockwell engineers to predict which components were most susceptible to failure before their predicted life. According to Robert E. Greer, president of Rockwell's B-1 Division at the time: *"The basic assumption in all fracture analysis is that cracks or crack-like flaws can exist in all structural components, and that they may grow due to load applications encountered in service. Our job has been to test thousands of combinations of metals to select exactly the right ones to use in the numerous fracture critical areas of the B-1, such as the wing carry-through structure, the supporting strut for the horizontal and vertical stabilizers and the tension skins on the wings."*

One of the most critical components of the B-1 is the wing carry-through structure, which connects the outer wings with their pivots. The carry-through must be tough enough to with-

stand the rigors of the wing sweep operation, while allowing the B-1 to operate at high speed and low altitude, where the Q (dynamic pressure) factors are high. The carry-through uses diffusion bonded 6AL-4V titanium alloy. This same material is also used for the wing pivot mechanism and the pivot pins. Titanium comprises 21 percent of the B-1 airframe. The sweep mechanism is activated by hydraulically operated screwjacks, with asymmetric movement prevented by a torque shaft between the two screwjacks.

The B-1A had a wingspan of 136 feet 8.5 inches (41.7 M) fully extended and 78 feet 2.5 inches (23.8 M) fully swept aft. The aircraft was 143 feet 3.5 inches (43.7 M) long, not including the 6 foot 11 inch (2.1 M) long test boom mounted on the nose of the first two B-1As. The B-1A stood 33 feet 7.25 inches (10.2 M) tall.

The B-1A carried 150,000 pounds (68,040 KG) of internal fuel in eight tanks: two in the wings and six in the fuselage. There is no accommodation for external fuel carriage. Weapons are carried in three 15 foot (4.6 M) long bays, two in front of the wing carry-through, and one aft. Each bay can accommodate approximately 25,000 pounds (11,340 KG) of a variety of nuclear and/or conventional ordnance. The empty weight of the B-1A was 140,000 pounds (63,504 KG), with a gross weight of 360,000 pounds (163,296 KG).

The aircraft was powered by four 30,000 pound thrust General Electric YF101-GE-100 turbofan engines with afterburning. These powerplants allowed the B-1A to reach a maximum speed of 1390 MPH (2236.9 KMH), or Mach 2.22, at 50,000 feet (15,240 M) altitude. Four men crewed the aircraft: Pilot, Co-Pilot, Defensive Systems Officer (DSO), and Offensive Systems Officer (OSO). The B-1A's unrefueled range was 6100 miles (9816.7 KM).

A serious problem for aircrews is the rough ride encountered at low altitude, due to constant turbulence. This can lead to fatigue and degraded crew performance on long legs at the B-1A's expected penetration altitudes. This is accentuated in an aircraft such as the B-1, with the crew sitting far forward of the Center of Gravity (CG). To dampen this effect, the B-1A was equipped with a Rockwell developed Low Altitude Ride Control (LARC) system – later renamed the Structural Mode Control System (SMCS). It is a derivation of two 'exciter vanes'

The first B-1A (74-0158) was rolled out of Rockwell's Palmdale, California plant on 26 October 1974. Test instrumentation was housed in the large, red-striped nose boom, which was only fitted to the first two B-1As. Large crew escape capsule stabilizing 'ears' are folded down on the fuselage side, above the title U.S. AIR FORCE. This aircraft and the three subsequent B-1As (74-0159, 74-0160, and 76-0174) were originally painted overall Gloss White (FS17875). (Rockwell)

that were mounted on the XB-70 research aircraft. SMCS uses two downward-canted vanes mounted on the aircraft's nose, which are activated by motion sensors in the fuselage. These sensors note accelerations in the airframe and move to damp out motions throughout all axis.

The first B-1A (serial number 74-0158) rolled out of Air Force Plant 42 in Palmdale, California on 26 October 1974. It made its first flight on 23 December 1974, with Rockwell test pilot Charlie C. Bock, Jr. in the left seat, Colonel Emil 'Ted' Sturmthal as co-pilot, and Richard Abrams as engineer. The flight delivered 74-0158 to Edwards Air Force Base (AFB), California for the start of flight testing. The number three aircraft (74-0160), configured as the avionics test bed, made its first flight on 26 March 1976. The number two aircraft (74-0159) was initially used as a static structural test article and did not fly until 14 June 1976. Because the political winds of change were swirling around the program in the late 1970s, the number four aircraft did not fly until 14 February 1979.

The B-1 team was cautiously optimistic when they began the formal flight test program in January of 1975. The only aircraft they would have for most of that year was the number one aircraft, so they proceeded carefully. The test program proceeded throughout 1975 and into 1976, while political trouble brewed in the person of Jimmy Carter. The Georgia governor won the Democratic nomination for president and then won the presidency in November of 1976, based in large part on promises to overhaul government, including the defense contracting process. During his campaign, Carter had referred to the B-1 as *"a wasteful program."* Although Rockwell was awarded a production contract for three additional airframes in December of 1976, this was followed by a titanic argument within the new administration over a full production decision for the now controversial bomber. USAF and Rockwell officials were hopeful that the new president would change his mind when confronted with the full real-ization of the Soviet threat that is afforded to the chief executive. In fact, they prepared for the President's B-1 news conference by having B-1 press kits on hand for attending journalists.

The announcement was made on 30 June 1977. Carter said: *"My decision is that we should not continue with the deployment of the B-1, and I am directing that we discontinue plans for production of this weapon system. The Secretary of Defense agrees that this is a preferable decision..."* Secretary of Defense Harold Brown had actually argued in favor of the B-1, but went along with the President's politically motivated decision to cancel the aircraft. (Carter had made cancellation of the B-1 a campaign issue.)

While he killed the B-1 production program, Carter allowed the testing and development program to continue. This was not much of a salve to the expectation of a production contract, which was to have totaled 240 aircraft, involving dozens of companies across the nation. It did keep open the possibility of a future production contract, should the alternative plan of improving B-52s and building wide-body cruise missile launchers prove insufficient to deal with potential threats. Rockwell immediately announced that it would lay off 16,000 workers, and Rockwell stock lost over 10% of its value before trading was halted.

The last of the four prototype aircraft (76-0174) made its first flight on 14 February 1979. It had entered production before the fateful cancellation, and took four years to complete. The four prototypes accumulated almost 1900 hours of testing flight time before the 30 April 1981 deadline for completion of the test program. While the test program was progressing, the Air Force continued to study possible replacements for its aging fleet of B-52s. The mission of a proposed follow-on bomber had evolved into more than that of cruise missile launcher or free-fall nuclear bomber. A multi-mission capable bomber was specified and on 2 October 1981, President Ronald Reagan announced that Rockwell would be awarded a contract to build 100 **B-1B** bombers.

The B-1 prototype is pulled out of the Palmdale factory. The first flight occurred from Palmdale on 23 December 1974. Two years of testing followed the initial flight in anticipation of a production decision in late 1976. The first B-1A was dedicated to flying qualities testing. It was the first B-1 to reach Mach 2, achieving this milestone in April of 1976. (Rockwell)

B-1A Crew Capsule
(Aircraft One through Three)

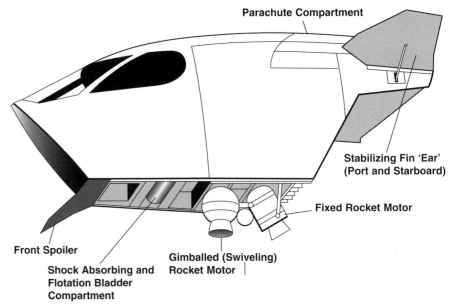

Parachute Compartment

Stabilizing Fin 'Ear'
(Port and Starboard)

Fixed Rocket Motor

Front Spoiler

Shock Absorbing and
Flotation Bladder
Compartment

Gimballed (Swiveling)
Rocket Motor

Overall white B-1As received the Strategic Air Command (SAC) insignia on a blue nose band with white stars. This aircraft was retrofitted with the blunter B-1B radome during the latter's flight test program in the early 1980s. B-1As were fitted with two air data probes on each side of the nose; the later B-1B has three such probes per side. (Lou Drendel)

A B-1A undergoes final assembly at Rockwell's Building 301 in Palmdale. The nose landing gear had a long drag brace leading from the main gear strut to the forward gear well. B-1B nose gears have shortened drag braces. The port crew escape module stabilizer 'ear' is raised. (Rockwell)

Composite material Structural Mode Control System (SMCS) vanes are mounted on both sides of the B-1's nose at a 30° anhedral (downward angle). The SMCS – called 'smucks' by 'Bone' crews – reduces oscillations caused by turbulence in flight, particularly at low level. This system helps prevent both airframe and crew fatigue. (Lou Drendel)

Air for the B-1A's four engines (two per side) was fed through variable geometry intakes, which featured adjustable intake ducts for meeting flight shock conditions. These intakes allowed the aircraft to reach Mach 2 speeds at high altitude. B-1A landing gear wheels were painted Gloss Black (FS17038), while struts and gear bays were Gloss White. (Lou Drendel)

A General Electric (GE) technician examines the first YF101 afterburning turbofan engine. The USAF selected this engine as the B-1A's powerplant in June of 1970. The YF101 generated 29,850 pounds of thrust in afterburner. The similar F101-GE-102 engine powering the later B-1B Lancer is rated at 30,780 pounds in afterburner. GE received a contract for 428 F101-GE-102 engines in 1982. (General Electric)

B-1A number one is parked on the ramp at Edwards AFB, California during the flight test program. Stabilizing 'ears' for the crew escape capsule are extended, permitting access to the central avionics compartment. These vanes automatically extended when the capsule was ejected. (Larry Davis)

The first B-1A (74-0158) flew profiles at 200 feet (60.96 м) above the ground during Terrain Following Radar (TFR) tests. A Texas Instruments AN/APQ-146 TFR – also used on the General Dynamics F-111F – was installed on B-1As. The General Electric AN/APQ-144 was the B-1A's main forward-looking radar. (USAF)

The third and fourth B-1As were modified with a dorsal spine in 1980. This spine contained the waveguide for the Kuras-Alterman 'Crosseye' Electronic Countermeasures (ECM) system. Both aircraft were painted in desert camouflage: Tan (FS30400), Green (FS34201), and Brown (FS30219), with Gloss White undersurfaces. The third B-1A (74-0160) retained the black radome. (USAF)

The number four B-1A (76-0174) was also painted in the desert camouflage, which covered the radome on this aircraft. The 'Crosseye' ECM system spine was later removed from the bomber and the waveguide incorporated into the fuselage. This B-1A – the first with ejection seats – later appeared in the three-tone 'Strategic Scheme' applied to B-1Bs. (USAF)

The third B-1A (74-0160) – complete with the 'Crosseye' spine and desert camouflage finish – is displayed at Edwards AFB, California. It was used for media tours in drumming up support for the B-1B program. After completing flight testing in April of 1981, this B-1A was retired to Lowry AFB, Colorado for service as a ground-loading trainer.

President Ronald Reagan resurrected the B-1 in 1981. The second B-1A (74-0159) was used as a B-1B test bed and received a new paint scheme for this duty. It was overall white with blue and red tail markings. The B-1 accompanies an NKC-135A refueling an F-15 Eagle during a test flight from Edwards AFB, California. (USAF)

The fourth B-1A (76-0174) is displayed at the USAF Museum, located at Wright-Patterson Air Force Base (AFB), Ohio. The large black and white circle on the engine nacelle side is a registration mark used for photo interpreting during test missions. Black wing root and vertical stabilizer leading edge panels house various antennas. (Lou Drendel)

B-1B Lancer

The decision to produce the B-1B was part of President Reagan's defense buildup initiative and a campaign promise. We now know that this program sounded the death knell for the Soviet Union and ended a 40 year cold war; however, it was little understood at the time. A national news magazine cited the *"unfathomable $1.5 trillion cost"* of the buildup, and was surprised that it was going ahead *"without any clear strategy."* They also questioned whether the defense industry would be able to *"deliver the new weaponry on time and within budget."* The B-1B portion of the proposed buildup was quoted at $2.4 billion. Initial B-1B contracts were let on 20 January 1982; $1.3 billion for the aircraft's full scale development and $886 million for tooling and production of the first B-1B. Rockwell was ready for the go-ahead and their B-1 program got underway almost immediately, benefiting from the $6 billion previously spent on study and testing. General Electric was also awarded contracts for producing 34,000 pound thrust **F101-GE-102** engines for this aircraft. There were 3000 sub-contractors involved in these contracts, and it was estimated that 58,000 jobs would be generated, including 22,000 at Rockwell.

The B-1B differed from the B-1A in several respects. The Radar Cross Section (RCS) was decreased by over 85% through engine inlet redesign. The change in the B-1's mission from high altitude penetration to low altitude had eliminated the Mach 2 speed requirement. This allowed a simplified intake design, eliminating the moveable air ramps used on B-1A intakes. RCS vanes placed within the inlets shield the engine faces from radar returns. The B-1B RCS is only 0.7 M^2 (7.5 sq. ft.) – less than two percent of the B-52's 70 M^2 (753.5 sq. ft.)

A B-1B test aircraft flies over southern California, accompanied by a civilian contractor's T-38 Talon (N638TC). The Lancer is finished in the 'Strategic Scheme' of Dark Gunship Gray (FS36081), Dark Green (FS34086), and Medium Gunship Gray (FS36118). The B-1 Combined Test Force (CTF) at Edwards AFB also used F-111, F-106, F-4, and F-15 chase aircraft during the B-1B testing and service acceptance flights. (USAF)

RCS. Simplified engine inlets reduced the B-1B's maximum speed from 1390 MPH (2236.9 KMH), or Mach 2.22, to 792 MPH (1274.6 KMH), or Mach 1.25, at 50,000 feet (15,240 M).

The B-1A's pointed nose radome was replaced by an ogival radome on the B-1B. A Westinghouse (now Northrop Grumman) AN/APQ-164 multi-mode offensive radar was fitted for navigation and terrain following use. This Synthetic Aperture Radar (SAR) enables B-1B crews to see their targets through heavy weather conditions. The crew escape module of the first three B-1As was eliminated (beginning with the fourth B-1A) in favor of conventional ACES (Advanced Concept Ejection Seat) II ejection seats. The four-man crew – Pilot, Co-Pilot, Offensive Systems Officer (OSO), and Defensive Systems Officer (DSO) – was unchanged from the earlier B-1A. The B-1B OSO and DSO each have a small window on the fuselage side, aft of the windshield. These windows were not installed on B-1As. The new variant has a more aerodynamic overwing fairing, which completely sealed the gap between the swept wing section and the aft fuselage. Fabric-covered rubber air bags seal the gaps between the wing sections and the upper and lower fairing surfaces. The aft fuselage was enlarged to accommodate increased defensive avionics. The B-1A's pointed tail cone and horizontal stabilizer fairing were changed on B-1Bs to those with a blunter shape, which allowed more volume for electronic equipment.

External dimensions for the B-1B are identical to the earlier B-1A. The wingspan is 136 feet 8.5 inches (41.7 M) fully extended (15° sweep angle) and 78 feet 2.5 inches (23.8 M) at full aft sweep (67.5°). Fuselage length is 143 feet 3.5 inches (43.7 M) and aircraft height is 33 feet 7.25 inches (10.2 M). Airframe strengthening for the low-level penetration role increased the B-1B's weight. The B-1A's empty weight of 140,000 pounds (63,504 KG) was increased to 192,000 pounds (87,091.2 KG) on the B-1B. The gross takeoff weight was increased from 360,000 pounds (163,296 KG) in the B-1A to 477,000 pounds (216,367.2 KG).

The second and fourth B-1A flight test aircraft (74-0159 and 76-0174) were modified to B-1B standard. The first flight of 74-0159 in the new configuration – although retaining the crew escape module – was from Edwards AFB on 23 March 1983. The fourth B-1A (76-0174) made its first flight in B-1B mode on 30 July 1984, carrying the full suite of B-1B offensive and defensive avionics. This aircraft flew in the B-1B test program until 31 October 1985.

One of the most critical aspects of the B-1 flight envelope is fuel load management. Fuel is distributed in six tanks located throughout the fuselage and one tank in each outer wing. Coupled with the ability to swing the wings, this can result in a radical shift in the Center of

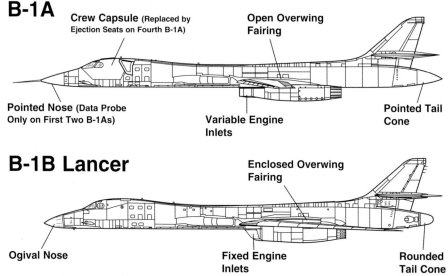

B-1A
Crew Capsule (Replaced by Ejection Seats on Fourth B-1A)
Open Overwing Fairing
Pointed Nose (Data Probe Only on First Two B-1As)
Variable Engine Inlets
Pointed Tail Cone

B-1B Lancer
Enclosed Overwing Fairing
Ogival Nose
Fixed Engine Inlets
Rounded Tail Cone

Gravity (CG). Production aircraft use fuel management computers to ensure the CG remains within limits. During a low speed handling test by the second B-1A on 29 August 1984, the schedule called for crew members to manage this task. After completing the first part of the test with the wings swept to 55° and the manual CG set at 45%, the aircraft was decelerated and wings swept forward. With the gear and flaps down, the test called for a CG setting of 21% at 138 knots (158.9 MPH/255.7 KMH). The crew failed to initiate fuel transfer and the CG remained at 45%. At 145 knots (167 MPH/268.7 KMH), the aircraft pitched up and apparently stalled, rolling to the right. Recovery attempts were made for the following 30 seconds before the crew pulled the ejection handle and the crew escape module fired. The aircraft impacted the ground nine seconds later. Unfortunately, the crew escape module did not function properly and Rockwell Chief Test Pilot T.D. Benefield was killed. Major Richard Reynolds and Capt Otto Waniczek were injured.

The first production B-1B (82-0001) rolled out of Rockwell's Palmdale plant five months ahead of schedule, on 4 September 1984, and made its first flight on 18 October. The first operational B-1B (named *The Star of Abilene*) was delivered to the 96th Bombardment Wing, Heavy (BMW) at Dyess AFB, near Abilene, Texas on 27 June 1985. The B-1B achieved Initial Operational Capability (IOC) in July of 1986 and stood its first nuclear alert the following 1 October. The final production aircraft was delivered to the Air Force in May of 1988, still ahead of schedule and under budget. The USAF officially christened the B-1B the 'Lancer' on 15 March 1990. Like most official names, the people who maintain and fly the B-1B have largely ignored it. They prefer the nickname 'Bone' (from B-One).

Lancers were originally delivered to four BMWs (Bomb Wings, BWs, from 1 October 1991): The 96th BMW at Dyess AFB; the 28th BMW at Ellsworth AFB, South Dakota; the 384th BMW at McConnell AFB, Kansas; and the 319th BMW at Grand Forks AFB, North Dakota.

Several B-1Bs, led by aircraft 22 (85-0062), are assembled at Air Force Plant 42 in Palmdale, California. The yellow chromate (approximately FS33481) primer coat prevented external surface corrosion. Rockwell produced all 100 B-1Bs between September of 1984 and January of 1988 – a rate of four aircraft per month. This was possible because of the extensive use of existing components. Rockwell assembled its B-1Bs in a new 922,000 square foot (85,653.8 M²) building at the Palmdale airport. (Rockwell)

The 100th and final B-1B (86-0140) is assembled at Palmdale. The Eaton AN/ALQ-161A Electronic Countermeasures System (ECMS) is installed at the vertical fin tip rear. Navigation lights are mounted under the antenna. The Lancer's rudder is divided into three sections, whose lower section has not yet been installed. This section is linked to the Structural Mode Control System (SMCS), working in conjunction with nose-mounted vanes to damp out airframe flexing in rough air. (Rockwell)

The final B-1B built rolls out of Palmdale's Plant 42 on 20 January 1988. A tractor tows the primer-coated Lancer to Rockwell's Automated Checkout Facility. The aircraft was painted and received final checks prior to its first flight. It was delivered to the 384th Bombardment Wing, Heavy at McConnell AFB, Kansas on 2 May 1988 – two months ahead of schedule. (Rockwell)

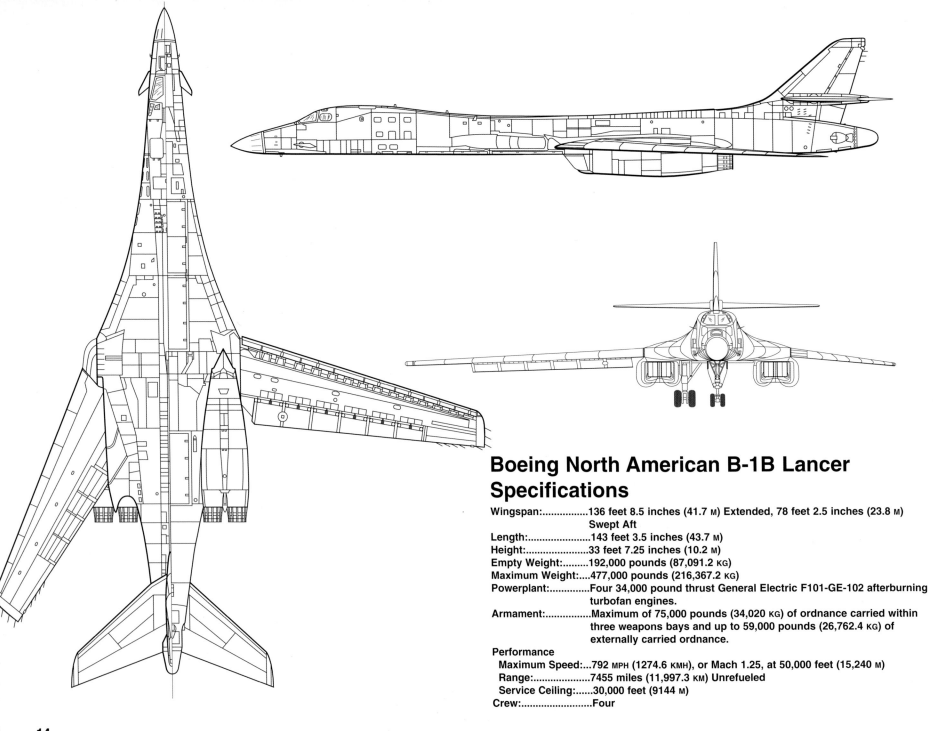

Boeing North American B-1B Lancer
Specifications

Wingspan:................136 feet 8.5 inches (41.7 M) Extended, 78 feet 2.5 inches (23.8 M)
Swept Aft
Length:......................143 feet 3.5 inches (43.7 M)
Height:......................33 feet 7.25 inches (10.2 M)
Empty Weight:..........192,000 pounds (87,091.2 KG)
Maximum Weight:....477,000 pounds (216,367.2 KG)
Powerplant:..............Four 34,000 pound thrust General Electric F101-GE-102 afterburning
turbofan engines.
Armament:................Maximum of 75,000 pounds (34,020 KG) of ordnance carried within
three weapons bays and up to 59,000 pounds (26,762.4 KG) of
externally carried ordnance.

Performance
  Maximum Speed:...792 MPH (1274.6 KMH), or Mach 1.25, at 50,000 feet (15,240 M)
  Range:....................7455 miles (11,997.3 KM) Unrefueled
  Service Ceiling:......30,000 feet (9144 M)
Crew:.........................Four

The B-1B engine intakes include Radar Cross Section (RCS) vanes in front of the engine faces. RCS vanes prevent radar reflections from hitting the engines and improve the Lancer's stealthiness. The B-1B also has reshaped overwing fairings, which offer improved aerodynamic performance over those fitted to earlier B-1As. Only the first B-1B (82-0001) had flutter wands on the horizontal stabilizer fairings for recording tip excursions – the amount of vertical flexing by the stabilizer tips. (USAF)

A B-1B undergoes ground testing at Palmdale in February of 1988. Hoses connect the 'Bone' to the fuel hydrant/Centralized Aircraft Support System (hydra/CASS). It supplies fuel, pressurized air, air conditioning, liquid coolant for avionics cooling, and electrical power to the aircraft. This underground system is installed at each parking spot on all B-1 operating bases, eliminating the need for multiple support equipment. (Rockwell)

The 96th BW was disbanded in 1993 and its assets assumed by the 7th Bomb Wing at Dyess. The 319th and 384th BWs were inactivated the following year. Other B-1Bs are assigned to the 34th Bomb Squadron at Ellsworth, which reports to the 366th Wing – the USAF's expeditionary wing – at Mountain Home AFB, Idaho. Two Air National Guard (ANG) units fly B-1Bs: the Kansas ANG's 184th BW at McConnell AFB, and the Georgia ANG's 116th BW at Robins AFB.

Not long after entering service, the B-1B demonstrated its performance through several record attempts. On 4 July 1987, the 58th B-1B (86-0098) set a new world speed record for a 2000 KM (1242.8 mile) circuit with a payload. It carried a 30,000 KG (66,137.6 pound) payload in a closed course along the California coast at an average speed of 1077.5 KMH (669.5 MPH). Simultaneously, this Lancer broke the Soviet Union's 1959 record for a 1000 KM (621.4 mile) closed course by flying at 1087.9 KMH (676 MPH). The 70th B-1B (86-0110) set the 5000 KM (3106.9 mile) speed record of 1054.1 KMH (655 MPH) on 17 September 1987.

On 28-29 February and 18 March 1992, two B-1Bs (86-0110 and 86-0121) of the 319th Wing from Grand Forks AFB set eight world time to climb records in three different weight classes. These ranged from 3000 M (9842.5 feet) in the C.1O Class (80,000 to 100,000 KG/176,366.8 to 220,458.6 pound) in one minute 13 seconds to 12,000 M (39,370.1 feet) in the C.1Q Class (150,000 to 200,000 KG/330,687.8 to 440, 917.1 pound) in nine minutes 42 seconds.

On 2-3 June 1995, two B-1s from Dyess AFB (84-0057 and 85-0082) completed a 36 hour and 13 minute around-the-world mission (Operation CORONET BAT). The 'Bones' covered 22,865.6 miles (36,797.6 KM) at an average speed of 631.16 MPH (1015.7 KMH). The speed record-setting flight also dropped bombs on practice ranges in Italy, Okinawa, and Utah to underscore the B-1s capability. Six mid-air refuelings were accomplished by the B-1Bs during this mission.

The 92nd B-1B constructed (86-0132) became the first 'Bone' to achieve 5000 flight hours on 9 May 2000. The entire B-1B fleet had accumulated 339,000 flight hours by April of 2001. Service life attrition was projected to be 2038, based on the Aircraft Structural Integrity Program (ASIP). The useful life of the structure is assumed to be the point at which it is more economical to replace the aircraft than to continue structural modifications and repairs necessary to perform the mission. The limiting factor for the B-1's service life is the wing lower surface. Based on continued low level usage, fatigue on the wing's lower skin at 15,200 flight hours will place the inventory below the 89 aircraft requirement in 2018.

After 15 years of operations, the B-1B remains one of the most sophisticated and effective weapons systems ever deployed. It is capable of flying intercontinental missions without refueling and can (and has) penetrated sophisticated enemy defenses to drop a larger payload of bombs than the load carried by its venerable predecessor, the B-52.

A B-1B flies in its designed element – low altitude at high speed. The white wing root navigation light operates when the wings are fully swept, while the wingtip navigation lights (red to port, green to starboard) work when the wings are fully forward. Wingsweep is normally between 65 and 67.5° in the transonic (0.8 to 1.2 Mach) range. This minimizes the effects of increased transonic drag, which occurs at approximately 0.85 to 0.9 Mach. (USAF)

The first B-1B (82-0001) taxies in takeoff configuration, with its hydraulically operated slats and flaps deployed to improve lift. Seven section leading edge slats extend first – down 20° – and retract last. The six section Fowler type trailing edge flaps have a maxi- mum deployment angle of 40°. Fairings on the horizontal stabilizer tips contained flutter wands not seen on other production 'Bones.' These wands collected information on the stabilizer's tip excursions (vertical flexing). (Rockwell)

The spoilers are deployed to the full 70° upward deflection on this 'Bone' parked at Dyess AFB, Texas. Spoilers are used to kill lift on landing and for sub-sonic roll control in the air. All four spoilers on each wing act as speed brakes on the ground, but only the two inboard spoilers per wing operate while airborne. B-1 horizontal stabilizers operate collectively (+10°/-25°) for pitch control, and differentially (+/-20°) for roll control. (Lou Drendel)

A B-1B takes off in full afterburner, powered by its four 34,000 pound thrust General Electric F101-GE 102 turbofan engines. The landing gear has retracted, although the main gear doors have not yet closed. Flaps and slats are retracted when the clean stall speed is reached and before the flap limiting airspeed is reached. Flaps retract in 20 seconds and slats retract sequentially in five seconds. (USAF)

The 'Bone' flies low altitude profiles in either Terrain Following (TER FLW) or Terrain Avoiding (TER AVD) modes. TER FLW provides inputs for flight pitch steering control at low levels, providing automatic let down and low altitude terrain following. TER AVD – used in conjunction with TER FLW – provides information on obstacles protruding above a clearance plane at a selected distance below the aircraft. This mode also displays areas of jamming, rain, towers, and a horizontal profile of the terrain at a given range. (USAF)

17

A B-1B refuels from a Boeing KC-135 Stratotanker. Fuel from the tanker is distributed to all eight tanks during refueling, and it is possible to exceed Center of Gravity (CG) limits when the forward fuselage tank (Tank 1) is full. CG excursions (unwanted short-term variations) from the Target CG are common during air refueling. The B-1B's Fuel Center of Gravity Management System (FCGMS) opens and closes the Tank 1 fill valves to maintain the Target CG during refueling. (USAF)

This B-1B (85-0068) performs at the airframe's maximum Gravity Force (G) limit in a wind-up turn during a test of the Stall Inhibit System (SIS). A combination of high G and high humidity creates a veil of condensation on the upper wing and fuselage surfaces. The SIS and a Stability Enhancement Function (SEF) were added to the B-1B as a result of increasing the maximum gross weight from 360,000 pounds (163,296 KG) in the earlier B-1A to 477,000 pounds (216,367.2 KG) in the B-1B. (USAF)

This B-1B (86-0105) is assigned to the 28th Bomb Squadron (BS), 7th Bomb Wing (BW) at Dyess AFB, Texas. The 28th BS is the training squadron for all B-1B crews. Operation CORONET BAT was flown by a pair of 7th BW 'Bones' in June of 1995. The two B-1s flew around the world non-stop in 36 hours and 13 minutes. The blue and white checkerboard tail flash was inherited from the former B-1 training unit, the 337th Combat Crew Training Squadron (CCTS). This Lancer is finished in overall Dark Gunship Gray (FS36081) with black markings. White refueling guide markings are applied to the nose. The nose art shows a cobra with two dice and the words SNAKE EYES. (Ted Carlson/Fotodynamics)

The B-1B nose landing gear can be steered 75° to port or starboard for directional control on the ground. The system is hydraulically operated and electronically controlled, with commands sent through the rudder pedals. Nose wheel steering is automatically disengaged when the landing gear is retracted. The landing gear track is 14 feet 6 inches (4.4 M) and the wheelbase is 57 feet 6 inches (17.5 M). (Rockwell)

Air conditioning hoses run to a 96th BW B-1B during extensive maintenance operations. The radome opens to port for access to the Westinghouse AN/APQ-164 offensive radar. The oval radar antenna provides the B-1B's crew with low altitude, terrain following, and precision navigation. Several port nose panels are opened for access to avionics equipment. (Rockwell)

The pilot's instrument panels are dominated by two large Cathode Ray Tubes (CRTs), which incorporate the Vertical Situation Display (VSD). VSDs show all flight data – including horizon, vertical speed, airspeed, ground speed, altitude, heading, and steering commands. Instrument Landing System (ILS) information is also displayed on the VSD. Backup 'steam gauges' (analog instruments) are grouped to starboard of the pilot's VSD. (Lou Drendel)

The co-pilot's panel and side console duplicates the pilot's controls and instruments. The large wing sweep control lever mounted above the side console is duplicated on the port side. A rear view mirror mounted above the lever knob provides visual verification of wing sweep. Large vertical displays flanking the VSD provide additional Airspeed/Mach and Altitude/Vertical Velocity information. (Lou Drendel)

The B-1B front cabin's center overhead panels includes the Air Refueling Control Panel, Auxiliary Power Unit (APU) Control and Indicator Panel, Electrical Power Control Panels, Main Lighting Control Panel, and Crew Compartment Pressure Altimeter. A standby compass is mounted at the vertical panel's center section, between the two air vents. Basic interior colors are Dark Gull Gray (FS36231) and Instrument Black (FS27038). (Lou Drendel)

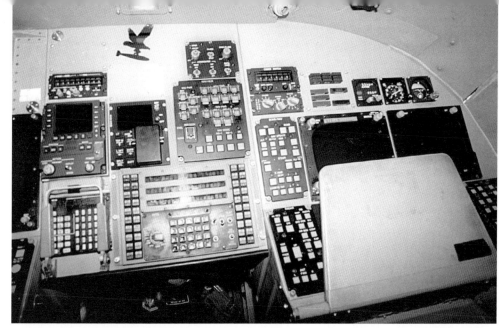

The B-1B aft cabin has crew stations for the Defensive Systems Officer (DSO, port) and the Offensive Systems Officer (OSO, starboard). The OSO's table is folded up when not in use. The central panel above the tunnel to the front cabin has controls for communications equipment and the Central Integrated Test System (CITS). CITS continually monitors the operation of all aircraft systems and displays malfunction data to the aircrew for mission capability evaluation. (Lou Drendel)

Both the DSO and the OSO have a small window mounted on the cabin wall. This window was not installed on the four B-1As. A circuit breaker panel is placed aft of the window. The gray track handle for controlling defensive systems is mounted beside the seat. The OSO has a similar handle for operating his systems. (Lou Drendel)

The DSO and other B-1 crewmen (since the fourth B-1A) each sit on a Boeing ACES II ejection seat. The seat fires upward immediately after a panel above the seat is jettisoned. Leg restraint straps are stowed by wrapping them around the ejection handles. These restraints pull the seat occupant's legs back against the seat, ensuring that they do not flail during the ejection sequence. The tunnel aft of the seat leads to the central avionics compartment. (Lou Drendel)

The B-1B's nose landing gear is similar to the earlier B-1A gear, although strengthened to handle increased aircraft weights. The drag link extending from the forward gear bay to the main strut is shorter on the B-1B. The nose gear retracts forward and upward into the fuselage, with emergency gear extension aided by the slipstream. The crew access hatch and retracting ladder is deployed aft of the nose gear strut. (Lou Drendel)

The four-wheel main landing gears appear similar to B-1A gears, but are strengthened to handle the B-1B's greater weight. The gear retracts inboard and aft into the fuselage. Multiple disk brakes are fitted to each wheel, and include an anti-skid system for braking on wet runways. B-1B landing gears and wells are Gloss White (FS17875) with chrome oleo (shock absorbing) struts. (Lou Drendel)

The B-1B uses fixed geometry engine inlets, which are simpler and less expensive than the B-1A's variable geometry inlets. This inlet features Radar Cross Section (RCS) vanes placed before the engine face enhance the Lancer's stealthy qualities by preventing radar returns from hitting the engine compressor. Hot air bled from the engines prevents inlet icing. (Lou Drendel)

Canvas-covered inflatable rubber bladders seal the gap when the B-1B's wings are swept back. It replaced a less aerodynamic fairing used on the earlier B-1A. The engine exhaust nozzle actuator fairings ('turkey feathers') were removed from Lancers during the early 1990s, saving weight and maintenance time. The exhaust nozzle controls the expansion ratio of the engine exhaust gas during all operations. (Lou Drendel)

Engine Intake Development

B-1A

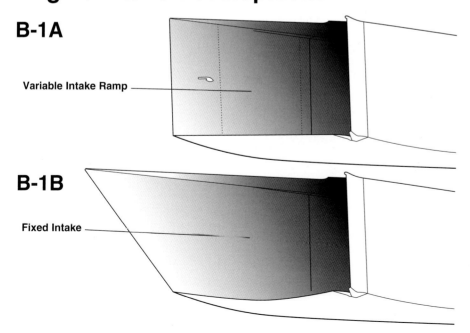

Variable Intake Ramp

B-1B

Fixed Intake

Overwing Fairing Development

B-1A   ## B-1B

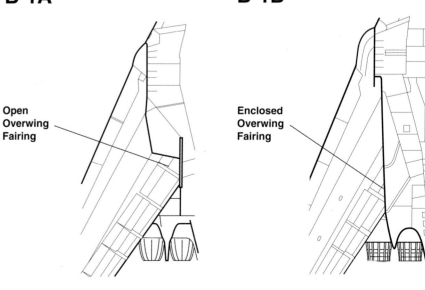

Open Overwing Fairing

Enclosed Overwing Fairing

This B-1B (85-0083) is assigned to the 77th Bomb Squadron ('War Eagles'), 28th Bomb Wing at Ellsworth AFB, South Dakota. The vertical fin tip fairing contains an ECMS antenna and the rendezvous radar beacon. A white tail light and an anti-collision strobe light are mounted below the fairing. Static discharge wicks attached to the rudder trailing edge dissipate static electricity from the airframe.

Eleven vortex generators per side are installed on the B-1B's aft fuselage and vertical fin. The vortex generators smooth airflow around the lower rudder, reducing fatigue and enhancing control surface effectiveness. If any of these items are missing, the Lancer is limited to subsonic speeds. RFS/ECMS defensive antennas are mounted on the tail cone sides and lower surfaces. The TDS has not been fitted to this Lancer. (Lou Drendel)

The B-1B replaced the B-1A's pointed tail cone with a blunter cone for housing the Radio Frequency Surveillance/Electronic Countermeasures System (RFS/ECMS) antennas. The horizontal stabilators operate differentially to provide supersonic roll control and operate in tandem to provide pitch control through all flight regimes. A large fairing mounted on the tail cone side houses the Towed Decoy System (TDS). The TDS includes the Raytheon AN/ALE-50 Airborne Expendable Decoy System. It is a programmable, computer-controlled, expendable countermeasures system controlled by the DSO. The TDS deploys an active Radio Frequency (RF) transmitter to redirect incoming missiles to the decoy. There are unconfirmed reports of a TDS saving a 'Bone' during operations over the Balkans in 1999. (Lou Drendel)

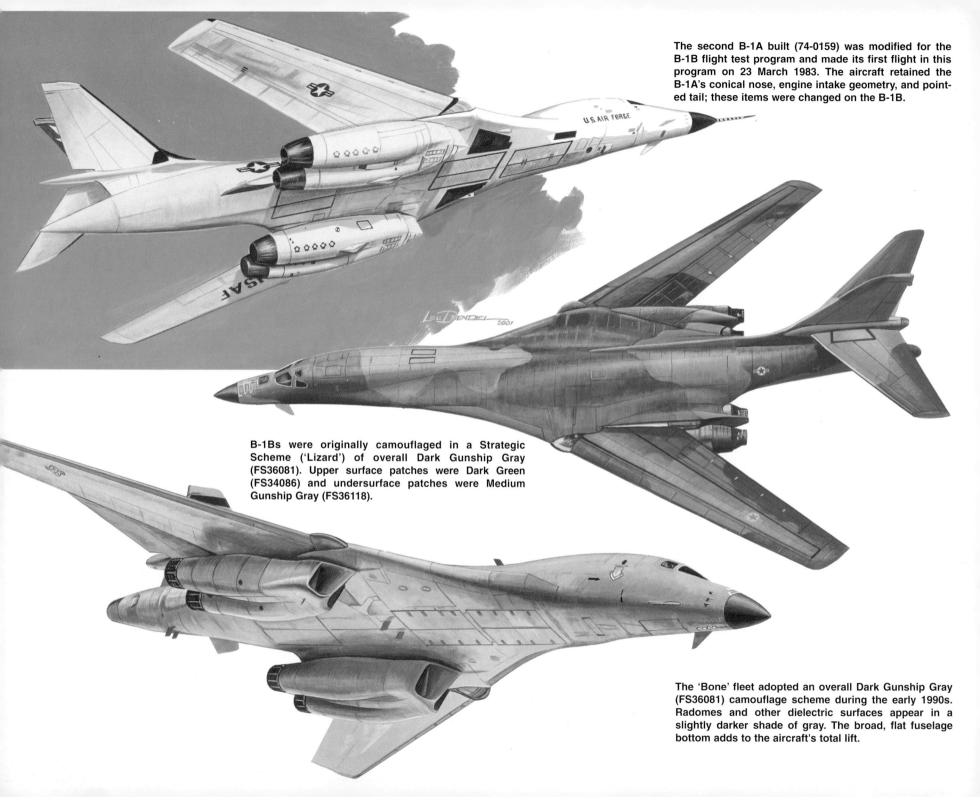

The second B-1A built (74-0159) was modified for the B-1B flight test program and made its first flight in this program on 23 March 1983. The aircraft retained the B-1A's conical nose, engine intake geometry, and pointed tail; these items were changed on the B-1B.

B-1Bs were originally camouflaged in a Strategic Scheme ('Lizard') of overall Dark Gunship Gray (FS36081). Upper surface patches were Dark Green (FS34086) and undersurface patches were Medium Gunship Gray (FS36118).

The 'Bone' fleet adopted an overall Dark Gunship Gray (FS36081) camouflage scheme during the early 1990s. Radomes and other dielectric surfaces appear in a slightly darker shade of gray. The broad, flat fuselage bottom adds to the aircraft's total lift.

BAD TO THE B-ONE (86-0107) was a B-1B assigned to the 9th Bomb Squadron (BS), 7th Bomb Wing (BW) at Dyess Air Force Base (AFB), Texas. The Squadron insignia is painted immediately aft of the nose art, while a white bat appears on the black tail stripe. In 1998, this 'Bone' was transferred to the 128th BS, 116th BW of the Georgia Air National Guard (ANG).

APOCALYPSE (85-0092) is a B-1B assigned to the 128th BS, 116th BW, Georgia ANG at Robins AFB. The aircraft was previously assigned to the 28th BW at Ellsworth AFB, South Dakota. The 116th BW is one of two ANG B-1B units, the other being the Kansas ANG's 127th BS, 184th BW.

Nearly all B-1 combat missions – over Iraq, Yugoslavia, and Afghanistan – have been flown at night. The pilot and co-pilot wear Night Vision Goggles (NVGs) clipped to their HGU-55P helmets on all night missions. The NVGs amplify available light to present an enhanced monochromatic view to the wearer.

B-1B Weapons

Although it was conceived as a long-range strategic nuclear bomber, the B-1 has evolved into a conventional attack platform. The Lancer can be armed with a wide variety of bombs, missiles, and mines. It can carry 75,000 pounds (34,020 KG) of ordnance internally in three weapons bays. The 'Bone' can also carry 59,000 pounds (26,762.4 KG) of externally-mounted weapons. External stations were designed for launching Boeing **AGM-86B Air Launched Cruise Missiles (ALCMs)** and have not been used operationally. Their use is problematic, since they add significantly to the B-1B's Radar Cross Section (RCS), thereby removing one of its primary defensive features.

The B-1's stated *raison d'être* (reason for being) was deep penetration of the enemy homeland with nuclear weapons. Compatibility testing was conducted from 1983 to 1990, with the B-1B eventually certified to carry **B61** and **B83** gravity nuclear bombs and Lockheed **AGM-69A Short Range Attack Missiles (SRAMs)**. Eight B61s, B83s, or AGM-69As were loaded in each weapons bay on a Multi-Purpose Rotary Launcher (MPRL). The USAF decided to restrict the B-1B to delivery of conventional weapons in 1991. In 1995, the Russians were allowed to inspect all Lancers to verify that their nuclear delivery capability had been removed to comply with treaty obligations. Arms control limits have resulted in the multi-part Conventional Mission Upgrade Program (CMUP), which transformed the Lancer into a conventional-only bomber since late 1997.

The most popular conventional weapons load is eighty-four 500 pound (226.8 KG) **Mk 82** bombs, with 28 bombs carried per weapons bay on a Conventional Weapons Module (CWM). The Mk 82 is a free-fall 'dumb' bomb, with three different fin sets available: 'Slick' (low-drag) conical fins, 'Snakeye' retard fins, and the BSU-49 Air Inflatable Retard (AIR) tail. The BSU-49 has a high drag or low drag mode, either of which can be selected in flight by the Offensive Systems Officer (OSO). Mk 82s use either proximity (radar) or mechanical fusing. This was the only non-nuclear bomb certified for use on the B-1B until 1995. The 28th Bombardment Wing, Heavy at Ellsworth AFB, South Dakota successfully completed Mk 82 certification trials on 21 July 1989.

The **Mk 84** is a 2000 pound (907.2 KG) version of the Mk 82. Each B-1B weapons bay can carry up to eight Mk 84s, mounted on an MPRL.

The **Mk 62 QS (Quick Strike)** mine is a derivative of the Mk 82 bomb, with a Mk 15 fin kit. The Mk 15 includes a drag parachute for slowing the mine's release from the aircraft to the water. The B-1 carries up to 84 of these bottom fused mines (28 per weapons bay) for use in water up to 300 feet (91.4 M) deep.

The Block C CMUP integrated three Cluster Bomb Units (CBUs) with the B-1B. The **CBU-87 Combined Effects Munition (CEM)** is a CBU carrying 202 bomblets. These bomblets are stabilized by a tail-mounted ballute (balloon/parachute), with an anti-material shaped charge in the nose, while the casing explodes into anti-personnel shrapnel. The B-1B can carry 30 CBU-87s – ten in each weapons bay.

The **CBU-89 Gator** is a 1000 pound (453.6 KG) CBU carrying 72 BLU-91/B antitank mines and 22 BLU-92B anti-personnel mines. The FZU-39/B proximity sensor detects enemy armor and explodes the mine at the optimum point. The anti-personnel mines are designed to eliminate mine clearing teams. The B-1B carries 30 CBU-89s.

The **CBU-97 Sensor Fused Weapon (SFW)** carries the SUU-66/B Tactical Munitions Dispenser (TMD), which releases ten parachute stabilized BLU-108/B sub-munitions. Each BLU-108/B contains five 5 inch (12.7 CM) armor penetrating projectiles with Infrared (IR) sen-

A Conventional Weapons Module (CWM) is prepared for loading aboard SPECTRE, a 7th Bomb Wing (BW) B-1B. The CWM is fitted with twenty eight 500 pound (226.8 KG) Mk 82 bombs. One module can be placed inside each of the Lancer's three weapons bays, allowing up to 84 bombs to be carried internally. CWMs have also been modified to carry ten Cluster Bomb Units (CBUs) and can also carry Mk 62 mines. (USAF)

Swing arms on the CWM hold bomb ejector racks, where ordnance is attached. The module is mounted on weapons bay trunnions, which also support rotary launchers. Bombs are released from bottom to top, with the bottom arms swinging clear when bombs are released to allow the next ejector rack to function. Weapons bay doors are fully open for CWM weapons release, but only partially open for releasing nuclear weapons. (Lou Drendel)

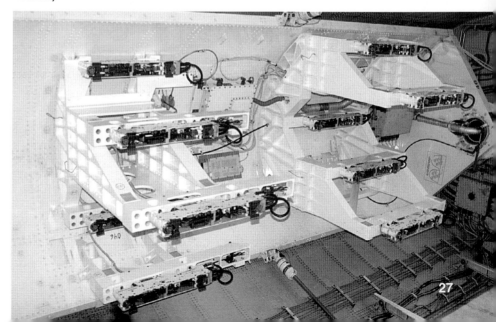

The two forward weapons bays are divided by a bulkhead, which may be moved or removed as required. It allows two 15 foot (4.6 M) long bays, one 22 foot (6.7 M) and one eight foot (2.4 M) bay, or a single 31 foot (9.4 M) bay. The trunnion mounted on the bulkhead supports either rotary launchers or CWMs. (John Gourley)

An empty CWM is installed inside the intermediate weapons bay. A perforated spoiler mounted on the bulkhead extends down when the bay doors open in flight. It reduces turbulence inside the bay and ensures clean weapons release. B-1B weapons bay interiors are Gloss White (FS17875). (Lou Drendel)

sors that detect enemy armor. The SUU-66 carries a radar altimeter. At a preset altitude, a rocket motor fires to spin the sub-munition and initiate its ascent. The sub-munition releases four projectiles, which are lofted over the target area. When the IR seeker senses a heat source, such as a tank engine, it fires a penetrator into the (presumably) soft armor on top of the tank. This sophisticated bomb carries a unit cost of $360,000. The B-1 can carry 30 CBU-97s, worth $10,800,000.

The Block D CMUP integrated the Boeing **GBU-32 Joint Direct Attack Munition (JDAM)**. It is a Global Positioning System (GPS)/Inertial Navigation System (INS)-guided version of the standard Mk 80 series gravity bombs. The fusing of the bomb remains the same, as does the casing and explosive. The guidance unit is contained in the tail assembly and can be fitted to any standard Mk 80 series bomb. The B-1B can carry twenty-four 2000 pound GBU-32 JDAMs, eight per bay, using the MPRL. Accuracy is within 45 feet (13.7 M) with active GPS guidance and 100 feet (30.5 M) without GPS. The bomb guidance unit receives position information via the aircraft system prior to release.

Block E CMUP upgrades include the Texas Instruments **AGM-154 Joint Standoff Weapon (JSOW)**, which uses a GPS/INS navigation system to lock on to its targets. It can be launched from as close as 17 miles (27.4 KM) at low altitude or 46 miles (74 KM) at high altitude. The AGM-154A carries the same sub-munitions as the CBU-87, while the -154B uses the same sub-munitions as the CBU-97.

The Lockheed Martin **AGM-158 Joint Air-to-Surface Standoff Missile (JASSM)** is a launch and leave cruise missile with a range of 200 miles (321.9 KM). It measures 168 inches (426.7 CM) long and weighs 2250 pounds (1020.6 KG), including the 1000 pound warhead.

The **Wind Corrected Munitions Dispenser (WCMD)** provides improved capability by adding the operational employment of WCMD variants of CBUs. An inertial guided WCMD tail kit assembly and a FZU-39/B proximity sensor are added to a CBU. The WCMD-converted CBU-87, -89, and -97 are designated **CBU-103**, **CBU-104**, and **CBU-105**, respectively. These weapons can be released from low or high altitude and are designed to attack armored formation targets and soft targets, day or night. A B-1B can carry 30 WCMDs, with ten weapons in each weapons bay. The dispensers are loaded on a Seventy-Sixty Enhanced Conventional Bomb Module (SECBM), which is placed in the bay.

Forward & Intermediate Stores Bays

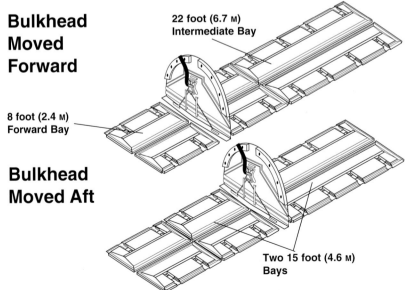

Bulkhead Moved Forward

22 foot (6.7 M) Intermediate Bay

8 foot (2.4 M) Forward Bay

Bulkhead Moved Aft

Two 15 foot (4.6 M) Bays

Inert CBU-89 'Gator' cluster bombs are loaded on a CWM installed in a B-1B. These training bombs have Dark Blue (FS35109) rings immediately aft of the nose. Each CBU-89 carries 72 BLU-91 anti-armor munitions and 22 BLU-92 anti-personnel munitions. These munitions are stabilized and detonated by proximity and/or Infrared (IR) sensors. The CBU-89 is similar in size to the CBU-87 Combined Effects Munition (CEM), whose bomblets explode into both anti-personnel and incendiary fragments. (Lou Drendel)

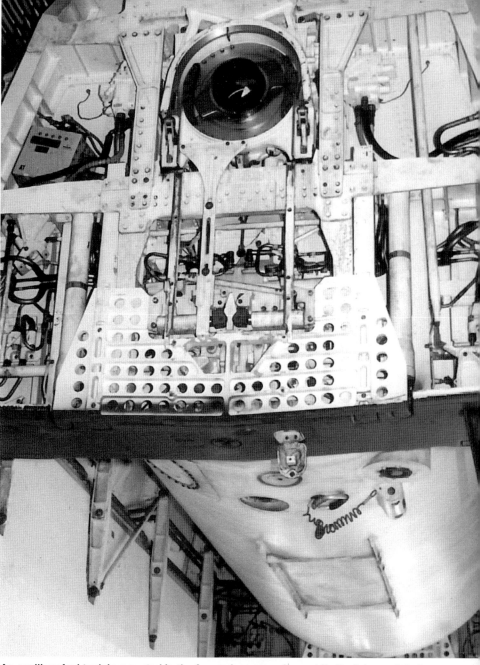

An auxiliary fuel tank is mounted in the forward weapons bay, while the intermediate bay is empty. Auxiliary tanks holding either 18,870 or 8352 pounds (8559.4 or 3788.5 KG) of JP-4 fuel can be loaded in the forward bay. The small capacity tank is loaded when the intermediate weapons bay is configured for cruise missile carriage. The 18,870 pound tank can also be installed in the intermediate and aft bays. (John Gourley)

A B-1B releases a full bay's worth of Mk 82 AIR bombs over the Edwards AFB bomb range in California. The ballute (balloon/parachute) tails retard the bombs' fall long enough to allow the B-1 to escape the fragmentation pattern at low altitude. Flying chase are an F-111 Aardvark (nearest the B-1) and an F-4 Phantom from the 6512th Test Wing at Edwards AFB. (USAF)

Mk 82 AIR bombs are fitted with BSU-49/B AIR fins. These bombs can be dropped in either high drag (ballute deployed) or low drag mode. Bomb release is controlled by the Offensive Systems Officer (OSO) from his station in the aircraft. The Mk 82 AIRs can be dropped from between 200 and 700 Knots Indicated Air Speed (KIAS). (Lou Drendel)

The intermediate weapons bay holds a full load of twenty-eight 500 pound Mk 82 Air Inflatable Retard (AIR) bombs loaded on a Conventional Weapons Module (CWM). AIR bombs can be released at higher airspeeds than bombs equipped with the earlier Snakeye folding fins. Nose plug fusing is used on AIR bombs. Inert Mk 82s used for training have blue nose bands. (Lou Drendel)

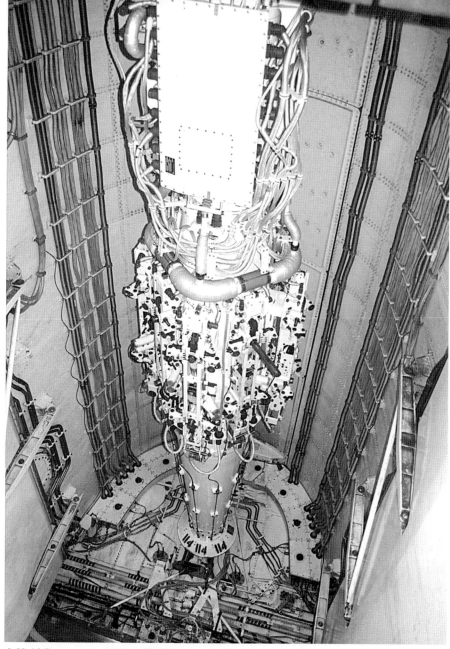

A Multi-Purpose Launcher (MPL) is mounted inside one of the weapons bays to drop up to eight conventional or nuclear weapons. The rectangular power control assembly is mounted on the launcher's forward end. Other rotary launchers were used for the AGM-69A Short Range Attack Missile (SRAM) and the AGM-86B Air Launched Cruise Missile (ALCM), until nuclear weapons capability was deleted from B-1Bs in 1991. (Lou Drendel)

Three inert 2000 pound (907.2 KG) Joint Direct Attack Munitions (JDAMs) are loaded on a rotary launcher mounted in a B-1B's forward weapons bay. The JDAM adds centerbody strakes and a new tail unit to the standard Mk 84 'iron' (conventional) bomb. A Global Positioning System (GPS) receiver in the tail guides the weapon to its target, through the four pivoting tailfins. Additional JDAMs are mounted in the intermediate weapons bay. (Lou Drendel)

B-1B at War

*War is a "continuation of political intercourse by other means." **Karl von Clausewitz***

Bill Clinton was one of the most political of all US presidents. Despite his professed distaste for the military and the use of force, he was far from reluctant to use the military for a variety of political reasons. Iraqi ruler Saddam Hussein was a most cooperative target, due to his continued disregard for the agreements reached at the end of the 1991 Gulf War. His program to develop weapons of mass destruction was kept out of the purview of United Nations inspectors. When the most vocal of these inspectors was expelled from the country, Clinton seized upon the opportunity to divert attention from his own political problems.

Operation DESERT FOX (December of 1998)
On December 16, 1998, United States Central Command (USCENTCOM) military forces launched cruise missile attacks against military targets in Iraq. These strikes were ordered by the President of the United States and were undertaken in response to Iraq's continued failure to comply with United Nations Security Council resolutions as well as their interference with United Nations Special Commission (UNSCOM) inspectors. The strikes were designed to deliver a serious blow to Saddam Hussein's capability to manufacture, store, maintain and deliver weapons of mass destruction and his ability to threaten or otherwise intimidate his neighbors.
By Linda D. Kozaryn
American Forces Press Service

Major Jeffrey 'Axel' Hoyt graduated from Kearny State College, Nebraska in 1985. He was newly married with no burning career plans when it occurred to him that flying aircraft might be fun. He walked into the local USAF recruiting office and signed up. Hoyt graduated from Officer Training School in 1987, pilot training in 1988, and B-52 training at Castle AFB, California in 1989. He flew B-52s until 1992, including one DESERT STORM (1991 Gulf War) mission. Hoyt began his B-1 training on 7 December 1992. He has been stationed at Dyess AFB since 1994 and has logged 1750 hours in the 'Bone.'

On 11 November 1998, Hoyt was notified that he would be deploying to Oman. He deployed on the 14th…but not to Oman. The plan, which was conceived as DESERT THUNDER, was put on a two-week hold. The first B-1s had arrived in Oman on 15 November, but all support equipment was held in Europe for a week, and Hoyt and his crew were held at Ellsworth AFB while the political options were explored. Hoyt finally arrived in Oman on 30 November, followed by a three-week period in which B-1 crews flew numerous training missions. On 15 December, all flight crews were stood down and notified that they would be flying operational missions. Iraq was attacked by cruise missiles the next day and the aircrews were alerted for missions the following night. The crew schedules were posted for the following week and the crews who were scheduled for the following night were instructed to begin their crew rest periods.

Although the 'No Fly' zones in northern and southern Iraq had been regularly patrolled since DESERT STORM and some anti-aircraft sites had been attacked, there had been no significant incursions flown since the Iraqi army had suffered the worst drubbing in modern warfare. The Iraqis had nearly eight years to build up their defenses; thus, the B-1 crews knew they would have to have their game faces on for the following night. They spent the night of the 16th watching CNN, then took the Flight Doc [Surgeon] prescribed sleeping pills and slept through

Two 28th BW 'Bones' are parked at Royal Air Force (RAF) Fairford, England during Operation ALLIED FORCE in 1999. The aircraft deployed from Ellsworth AFB, South Dakota to Fairford for the NATO air campaign over Kosovo between 24 March and 7 June

1999. Nine different B-1Bs took part in the operation, although no more than six aircraft were based at Fairford at any one time. The Lancers – and B-52s also deployed to Fairford – attacked strategic targets in Yugoslavia. (via Jeff Warmka)

the day. Hoyt recalls:

"We were a part of a Naval Package, and it was the first time a bomber had been in Iraq since DESERT STORM. The target was the Republican Guard barracks in Al Kut [approximately 95 miles (152.9 KM) south-southeast of Baghdad]. *(The Republican Guard is the elite unit, which owes personal allegiance to Saddam Hussein and is the primary instrument of his tyranny.) It was in what we called the 'Supermis'...the Super Missile engagement ring, with plenty of triple A* [Anti-Aircraft Artillery], *known SAM 2 and 3* [Soviet-built V-75 Dvina and S-125 Neva Surface-to-Air Missile] *sites and suspected SAM 6 and 8* [Soviet-built Kub and Romb SAM] *sites. Despite these known threats, we felt more confident than we had prior to DESERT STORM.*

"Before DESERT STORM, there was a great deal of apprehension. Iraq had the fourth largest standing army, including a very sophisticated integrated air defense system. In the briefing prior to the first night of DESERT STORM, B-52 crews on Diego Garcia [an island in the Indian Ocean] *were told; 'Look around, because a third of you are not coming back.' But because our air campaign was so well thought out and so well executed, we pretty much knocked their eyes and ears out right away, and for the balance of the campaign the Iraqi air defense was forced to operate autonomously. As you know, they were largely ineffective.*

"Prior to DESERT FOX, we had eight years of experience of operating against their defenses, but the Iraqis also had eight years of experience. We knew that they had decentralized and had given local commanders the discretion to fire at will. So, while we were confident, we were also mindful that we could face some surprises. The Iraqis, of course, are always fearful of taking a HARM [AGM-88 High Speed Anti-Radiation Missile] *down the throat, but we knew that we were presenting them with a target that might inspire some gunner to risk taking a HARM in the snotlocker* [nose] *to be a hero to his countrymen. This was the first combat for the B-1, a heavy bomber and a pretty high profile one at that, so we knew this was not going to be a cakewalk.*

"We showed at 2200 [hours] *on the night of the 17th, took about 30 minutes to study the package, and then spent an hour in the briefing. The package consisted of an AWACS[1]* [E-3 Sentry], *two B-1s, two F-14s, one EA-6B, six F-18 Strikers* [attack aircraft], *and two F-18s devoted to suppression of air defenses. Political constraints dictated that the Navy was assigned to the escort and air defense roles, while we carried the majority of the bombs. (Saudi Arabia would not allow basing of offensive aircraft, so the shorter range fighters came from carriers, while the longer range B-1s came out of Oman. AWACS never left Saudi airspace, so they were allowed to fly.)*

"The whole operation was designed to create a rift between the regular army and the Republican Guard, and the main objective was the Al Kut Barracks complex. Leaflets had been dropped in the days preceding the mission, emphasizing that our quarrel was not with the regular Iraqi army units, but that we were going after Republican Guard units. Each B-1 carried 63 Mk 82 500 pound bombs.

"At about 2130 we went to Life Support to draw our survival gear. My Co-Pilot was 1/Lt Bob Mankus, the Offensive Systems Officer (OSO) was Capt Gordon Greaney, and Capt Jason Xiques was in the Defensive Systems Officer (DSO) seat. These were three of my best friends

[1]AWACS: Airborne Warning And Control System. This aircraft is equipped with radar for controlling friendly fighters against enemy aircraft.

A B-1B assigned to the 77th BS, 28th BW awaits its load of 500 pound (226.8 KG) Mk 82 bombs at RAF Fairford during the spring of 1999. These 'dumb' (unguided) bombs comprised the majority of weapons used by Lancers during ALLIED FORCE. B-1Bs also released some Precision Guided Munitions (PGMs; 'smart bombs') on Yugoslav targets. (via Jeff Warmka)

An armorer loads a Mk 82 bomb aboard a B-1B at RAF Fairford. The weapon is placed on an MJ-1 lift truck for delivery to the aircraft. The Lancer's wings are usually set fully forward (15˚) while on the ground, facilitating taxiing and takeoff. During Operation ALLIED FORCE, Fairford B-1s operated with the call signs of *Bone, Razor, Foil, Havoc, Titus,* and *Yard*. (via Jeff Warmka)

Armorers load an empty Conventional Weapons Module (CWM) aboard a 'Bone' at Fairford. CWMs can be pre-loaded with ordnance prior to installation; in practice, they are most often loaded empty, then fitted with bombs. During Operation ALLIED FORCE, all CWMs were in the conventional '28 carry' configuration, with twenty-eight 500 pound Mk 82 bombs. (via Jeff Warmka)

as well as members of my crew. This was the normal routine, but an additional detail brought home to us that this was not a routine mission. We drew personal weapons and ammunition for our survival vests. The 'Bread Truck' [crew van] took us to our airplanes.

"The line was swarming with maintenance crews, and they had done a superb job in getting the airplanes prepped for the mission in a relatively short period of time. I was assigned to 86-[0]135. I had flown this jet for years, and it was my favorite...even before this mission, it was my favorite jet. SSgt Andy Pitts was crew chief, and I knew that if I got this jet it was going to be good to go. I had known most of the maintenance troops for years too, and they were proud of the work they did. We noticed that they had decorated the bombs with various bad wishes for Saddam's boys.

"We went through the normal preflight and pre-start routines and the jet came up quickly without a single problem. Our flight lead, from the 37th Bomb Squadron out of Ellsworth AFB, did have a problem, and he had to switch to another jet. They finally got their jet on line and we taxied out and took off. We couldn't know it at the time, but the entire flight line was filled with cheering troops. Would have been nice to see, but I'm glad I was where I was right then.

"Our route was the same one we had flown in a practice mission the previous week. It is 'Blue Two' low level route, and having just flown it, I knew when I was going to be talking to Omani controllers, when I would have dead airspace, then the British controllers working for the United Arab Emirates, Bahrain Control, then out over the Persian Gulf, where we checked in with the Navy controllers. We arrived at our orbit point on time, and waited for the Navy airplanes to take off and come up to their air refueling points. There were two **KC-10** tankers tasked with refueling the Navy jets, and we could see the lights off in the distance as they went around in the AR track, filling up.

"We orbited for 45 minutes while the Navy mission commander got his assets refueled and ready to push in-country. Right on time, we rolled out and headed for our target. We were on Night Vision Goggles (NVGs), so we were able [to] keep sight of everybody. The mission commander had decided not to entirely black everyone out, so we all had minimum lighting. NVGs cast a greenish pall over everything and all lights have a halo on the NVGs. If you see a light that is moving, that is another aircraft. Depth perception, of course, is very bad and we do not fly off of each other visually at night. We fly in a radar static position. The NVGs are positioned on your head so that if you move your eyes outside, you are looking through the NVGs. If you look down, towards the instrument panel, you are not looking through the NVGs. Even though we don't fly visually at night, the NVGs give us an added advantage of being able to pick out stuff you would never see in the dark.

"We overflew Kuwait, heading for Tallil in southern Iraq. We turned away from Tallil, still heading in the general direction of Baghdad. As we made this turn (south-southeast towards Al-Kut), we heard the EA-6 fire a HARM missile at an SA-6 battery in Tallil. This missile site was on a major highway that we were going to have to cross. We were going to pass very close to the confluence of the Tigris and Euphrates Rivers, and Gordon was using the major river crossing bridge as a radar checkpoint. I could hear Gordon and Jason in the back, exclaiming about how great the radar picture was...how well it came in...and I thought; 'Geez guys, one of our jammers [Electronic Countermeasures (ECM) aircraft] just shot a HARM at a no-kidding enemy missile site. This is not a training mission!' I warned them to get back in the ball game, but then thought that this sure was like a training mission in the way it was all going according to the plan.

"About that time, I could begin to see the lights of Baghdad. It was just like any other major metropolitan area, ablaze with light. It reminded me of flying around Dallas-Fort Worth. I remember thinking, 'Man, I sure don't want to fly into that!' The plan was to feint like we were going to Baghdad, then turn and hit Al Kut. The route had been programmed into the Offensive System and the jet was on autopilot, while Bob and I kept checking to make sure we stayed on course. The fighters turned off early to go to their targets, and that left us between our fighters and Baghdad, and that left us hoping there were no Iraqi fighters airborne. (There weren't)

"We got to the IP [Initial Point[2]] and Gordon was able to get a great offset radar picture of the target. The barracks narrowed down to a point, and our two B-1s were approaching from slightly different headings to make sure we marched the bombs across the target, meeting at the point. As I rolled into the turn towards the target, Bob said; 'There it is!' I said; 'There what is?' 'The triple A!' He was looking down, and could see over the nose, while I was on the high side of the turn and couldn't see it. As soon as I rolled out, I saw it. The Iraqis knew we were coming, and they had started shooting as soon as the fighters dropped their bombs.

"The way it worked...as soon as somebody dropped a bomb within earshot, all the gunners opened up. None of this fire was guided, but it was pretty impressive anyway. They hoped that someone would fly through some of their fire and get hit, but we were above practically all of what they were shooting.

"Now back on autopilot, we just waited to get to the bomb release point. The doors opened, and bombs came out, right on target. Since we were now in a combat environment, I pulled the maximum allowable G in the turn off the target, heading back south, and called mission successful.

"We had lost sight of the lead B-1 and could not pick him up on radar, though we knew he was out there. Up to that point, everyone in the package had been very disciplined about staying their lanes, but now that we were off the targets, everyone was just; 'Hey, we're outta here!' I asked the lead to turn on his lights momentarily, and then we picked them up at our 10:30 [just off the port nose]. I had turned inside of him coming off the target. We got back in position and continued south.

"Both B-1s had bombs left. We had 19 (two in the forward bay and 17 in the mid-bay) and lead had 20. This happened because of the fail-safe design of the ejector racks. The bombs are really packed in to the bays and swing arms must move out of the way before the set row of ejectors is cleared to drop. If they don't move quickly enough, the computer shuts the system down to make sure that the bombs don't collide with each other.

"This was not an unanticipated problem and we had been briefed on a 'dump target' in the Southern 'No Fly' zone. It was an old Iraqi airfield, which had not been used since DESERT STORM. Gordon picked out the target on radar, and found two hangars at the southeast edge of the airfield. Fifteen of our remaining bombs came off and found that target. We ended up with four bombs that we could not drop.

"The only threat indication we got on the whole mission came shortly after this. As we approached the Kuwaiti border, Jason came up; 'Pilot! I have an SA-2 at 4 o'clock!' [Off the starboard side – ed.] We called this threat to flight lead, maneuvered right and accelerated out of the threat area. Within a minute we were back over Kuwait and heading for home. We had taken off at 0100, and would be landing about an hour after sunrise, at 0700. The sun came up on a beautiful, clear day.

"Since both of us had retained weapons, we had to declare an emergency. An additional glitch occurred when lead did not get a safe gear down indication. We closed back up on him and visually checked the gear. It appeared to be down, but we were cleared to land first anyway, just in case. We landed to the north, while he landed to the south, so there were B-1s at

[2]Initial Point: The starting point for a bomb run.

A Mk 82 bomb is hoisted aboard a swing arm on a CWM loaded aboard a B-1B. Two lugs on the bomb's upper surface are captured by an ejector rack, which is installed on one of the CWM's four swing arms. Ejector racks must be cleaned and reloaded before weapons can be reloaded on the CWM. Bombs are overall Olive Drab (FS34087) with Orange-Yellow (FS33538) nose rings on conventional explosive weapons. (via Jeff Warmka)

Captain Jeff Warmka of the 77th BS, 28th BW accepts his 'Bone' from TSgt Pat Johnson at Ellsworth AFB. Soon after signing the paperwork, Warmka deployed to RAF Fairford for Operation ALLIED FORCE on 31 March-1 April 1999. He flew 17 'counters' (missions reaching the Adriatic Sea) during NOBLE ANVIL, the US component of ALLIED FORCE. (via Jeff Warmka)

This load of Cluster Bomb Units (CBUs) was fitted to a CBM, but was never dropped. Many ALLIED FORCE missions were briefed and flown without ordnance being dropped, for a variety of reasons. Ground crews at Fairford continued the tradition of writing never-to-be-read messages to the targets. Chalked on one CBU was: THIS IS THE LAST DAY OF YOUR LIFE. HOPE YOU ENJOYED IT. (via Jeff Warmka)

either end of the runway, shut down while the armorers made sure the weapons were safed. The jets were towed to parking, which was kind of a let down. B-1s flew an additional mission the following night [18 December]*, then the operation was shut down."*

DESERT FOX was the B-1's combat debut. It would be followed within a few months by a more extensive employment of the 'Bone' in combat over Kosovo, one of the provinces of the former Yugoslavia.

The collapse of the Soviet Union in the early 1990s created many political vacuums in several former Eastern Bloc countries. The former Yugoslavia reverted to internecine warfare between provinces with long-standing political, religious, and ethnic grievances against one another.

The Kosovo crisis started in early 1998 with fighting between regional factions and the Serb-dominated army of the Federal Republic of Yugoslavia. The widespread and vicious battles resulted in the displacement of over 300,000 people. Despite agreement on a cease-fire in October of 1998, fighting continued and the situation worsened in early 1999. Diplomatic efforts to end the war continued with a Paris Peace Conference, which ended in March without agreement on a peaceful solution.

Operation ALLIED FORCE was a North Atlantic Treaty Organization (NATO) response with the stated objectives of ensuring full compliance with UN Security Council Resolution 1199 (23 September 1998). Operation NOBLE ANVIL was the American component of this NATO action and began on 19 March 1999. Unlike Operation DESERT STORM, which was a textbook application of airpower that quickly achieved the objectives of degrading the enemy, ALLIED FORCE reverted to the Vietnam strategy of graduated pressure. Predictably, ALLIED FORCE failed to discourage the Serbian Army and thousands of additional ethnic Albanians and Kosovars died or were displaced before NATO shifted its focus from tactical targets to strategic targets. The latter targets included command and control facilities in the Yugoslav capital, Belgrade.

In DESERT STORM, coalition forces flew 40,000 strike sorties[3] in 30 days. In ALLIED FORCE, NATO flew 9000 sorties in 78 days. Precision-Guided Munitions (PGMs), or 'smart bombs,' comprised 70% of the bombs dropped in ALLIED FORCE. B-52s and B-1s dropped the remaining 30% of bombs expended during this campaign. Although only four B-1s were tasked at any one time, they dropped 45% of the gravity or 'dumb' bombs, all of which were 500 pound (226.8 KG) Mk 82 weapons.

Six B-1s from the 77th Bomb Squadron (BS) and two from the 37th BS – both of the 28th Bomb Wing from Ellsworth AFB, South Dakota – were assigned to the 100th Air Expeditionary Wing at Royal Air Force (RAF) Fairford, England. They shared the base with 18 B-52 bombers from 2nd and 5th Bomb Wings. Prior to their deployment, there was some consideration given to flying the missions from Ellsworth. These would have been 30-hour missions, versus the 7-hour mission time from Fairford. Ultimately, the convenience of home basing was overcome by the fatigue of 30-hour missions.

Captain Jeff Warmka is a 1992 graduate of the US Air Force Academy. His first operational assignment was to the B-1, joining the 37th BS at Ellsworth AFB in 1996. When the 77th BS was reactivated in 1997, Jeff transferred from the 37th to the 77th.

He was at the forefront of the deployment for ALLIED FORCE, leaving Ellsworth for RAF Fairford on 31 March 1999. The first B-1 missions were flown on 1 April. During NOBLE ANVIL, the American segment of ALLIED FORCE, Jeff flew 17 'counters.' (Combat mis-

[3]Sorties: A sortie is one operational mission flown by one aircraft.

sions were only counted if the flight reached the Adriatic Sea. Several missions were recalled, for a variety of reasons, prior to reaching this benchmark.) He had been flying missions for a month when he was assigned to what would become his most memorable mission of the deployment.

The Novi Sad petroleum production facility in northern Yugoslavia was a vital producer of oil for the Serbian war machine. This made it a high value strategic target, but the initial objectives of ALLIED FORCE were limited to the destruction of tactical targets. When it became apparent that tactical warfare alone was not going to stop Serbian aggression, the target list was expanded to include infrastructure like Novi Sad, which was a perfect target for area bombing. No other aircraft in the inventory could fly an area bombing mission like the B-1, so the 77th got the assignment on 1 May 1999. This is Jeff's recollection of that mission, which proved to be more exciting than most:

"Our sortie prep[aration] *was standard, which meant an afternoon show* [briefing] *at the operations building, where the mission planning cell had worked on everything and pretty much put the plan together while we were in crew rest. They briefed us on the mission package after we spent some time reviewing the paperwork. The package was comprehensive and included ingress and egress routes, [and] a copy of the Air Tasking Order* (ATO), *which included everyone who would be flying that night."*

'Integrated Air Defense' is a well-worn term that applies to a network of enemy anti-aircraft weapons. It was the way the Allies went about attacking Kosovo. Attack packages consisted of fighter bombers – often from several different air arms – 'Wild Weasel' HARM shooters, jamming platforms, air-to-air Combat Air Patrol (CAP) fighters, AWACS, and tankers in addition to the heavy bombers.

"Quite a few of the strikers were scheduled to hit their targets before us. This was due to the fact that after we hit the target, it would be pretty much obscured in dust, flames and smoke from our combined load of 168 Mk 82 500 pound bombs. Most of our strike packages consisted of US aircraft only. Practically all of my missions were flown as part of a combined package.

"From an historical standpoint, Novi Sad was a good bomber target. It was a large production facility, with good radar definition. We were able to drag an 1800-foot [548.6 M] *long string of bombs across the target and have virtually every one of the bombs hit something worthwhile. Though it had been hit a couple of the nights previously, it was still operating. Our plan was to flow through the target, then turn north to our 'dump target' to get rid of any weapons which had not come off on the Novi Sad run. The mission planning cell had done a good job on the package, and we were confident as we stepped out to the jet in the late afternoon sun.*

"It was still daylight when we took off into a clear sunset. The climb out was uneventful and before long the full moon was up, and it was so bright that we could see the Italian Alps without the aid of the Night Vision Goggles that we wore on every mission. We crossed Italy and pushed into the Adriatic. The radios were busy, like they were on most nights, and there was some initial confusion about the frequency we were supposed to work, but AWACS eventually straightened it out and we checked in with the F-16 SEAD (Suppression of Enemy Air Defenses) *flight. We marshaled to the west of the target, and when the package was together, we headed for the IP* [Initial Point].

"The weather was good, with just a few cumulus [dense white] *clouds over the target, and we could see the target from a long ways out. As we approached the IP, we began to pick up some AAA* [Anti-Aircraft Artillery]. *It seemed close, but was well below us. The F-16s*

This 77th BS B-1B (85-0091) is parked at Ellsworth AFB in August of 1999, following combat over Yugoslavia. The 'Bones' flown during Operation ALLIED FORCE were the first Lancers equipped with the Towed Decoy System (TDS) on the tail cone sides. The TDS employs the ALE-50 radio frequency repeater jammer against enemy missiles aimed at the B-1. (Lou Drendel)

Twenty-five Kosovo War combat mission markers are painted on the nose landing gear doors of this 77th BS B-1B. The insignia is a black silhouette of the Squadron's War Eagle mascot with a bomb in its talons. Red streamers with REMOVE BEFORE FLIGHT in white are attached to nose gear locks, which prevent inadvertent gear retraction while the B-1B is on the ground. (Lou Drendel)

A CWM with Mk 82 bombs is loaded in a B-1B's weapons bay at Fairford. The bombs are equipped with M904 instantaneous fuses in the noses, allowing detonation upon contact with the target. A computer software interlock in the CWM's logic unit prevents weapons from being released from higher stations until the preceding weapon has cleared the bay. (via Jeff Warmka)

responded quickly. It seemed like they knew right where we were, but that was probably just because we had been attacking night after night after night, and they had just come to expect it. The primary threat to us was SAMs. The AAA couldn't really reach our altitude, and our MIGCAP [MiG Combat Air Patrol] was so effective that the air-to-air threat never materialized. The SAM threat was pretty well negated by our HARM shooters. If an enemy radar was turned on, he could expect a HARM down the throat in short order. Those HARM shots sometimes created an adrenaline jolt in other airplanes. When you see a missile shot at night, it is very bright, and it is not always easy to tell if it is outgoing or incoming.

"The **F-15E** flight was also attacking Novi Sad. We were familiar with their timeline and it was reassuring to see their bombs impacting the target, right when and where we expected them to be. We were the last to hit the target, and we flowed through on schedule. The majority of our weapons came off and walked right through the target. Coming off, we made the off target calls to the other package players, then turned North towards our dump target.

"We could hear all the other package players on the radio...there was still a lot of triple-A and the F-16 SEAD jets were still doing their thing. I looked back at the target area, and it was just a sea of explosions and towering billows of smoke. We continued to see a lot of triple-A at what I estimated to be mid-level altitudes, though that is kind of hard to verify, since the Night Vision Goggles we wear tend to make it a 2-D [Two-Dimensional] environment. What you gain in visibility, you lose in depth perception. Hammer Flight, the SEAD F-16s, called that they were rolling in on the Triple-A sites.

"At this point, I heard one of the F-16 pilots call that he was 'defensive' in a very strained voice. There were a couple of SAM shots, one of which appeared to guide and explode, while the second one burned out and went ballistic. They were followed in short order by a pair of HARM shots.

"Hammer Lead called for check-in and standby. The number four guy called that he had a problem. He said: 'I'm heading West; I'm a glider; Trying to restart the engine.' What had been a strained voice trying to avoid the SAMs, was now a very calm, matter-of-fact voice dealing with the ultimate emergency. (Engine-out, over the heads of folks you have recently been bombing.) The rest of the guys in his flight were coordinating with the rescue forces, trying to pin down his position, and generally providing whatever support they could over the radio. While we couldn't see any of this drama, the radio transmission provided a real-time play by play. It was pretty amazing listening to all this...the professionalism of the players, from the guy going down, through all of the folks who were dedicated to getting him out, was really impressive.

"His last transmission was: 'I'm getting out boys, come and get me!' Through my NVGs, I saw the flash from his ejection seat, then the explosion as his F-16 hit the ground and blew up. We were apparently the closest to this, because there was some question about whether or not he actually got out. I was able to confirm that he had ejected.

A 'Bone' crew stands before their aircraft at Fairford. Mission markings on the nose gear door upper edge indicate seven missions on which bombs were dropped (eagle with bomb), and four on which no ordnance was dropped (eagle without bomb). Markers on the lower edge indicate four Serbian MiG-21 fighters destroyed during a raid on Pristina airfield, Kosovo on 4 April 1999. (via Jeff Warmka)

"Everyone in the package wanted to stick around and help with the rescue, but most of us would have just been in the way, so after a couple of orbits, we headed west. Ironically, there was a mix of emotion. We were angry that they had been shooting as us, and had actually gotten one of our guys. We wanted to load up and go right back to bomb them some more! Of course, they were just defending their territory and you really couldn't blame them for that. We met up with our tankers and three hours later we were back at Fairford. We were relieved to learn that the F-16 pilot had been picked up and returned to his base by the time we landed.

"All of our missions were flown at night, and in just about all weather. We didn't often see the immediate results of our efforts. What made this mission so memorable was being able to see so much. A combination of an area target, clear weather, full moon, and a lot of varied action pre and post-target almost made us feel like spectators as we watched the mission unfold."

NOBLE ANVIL was the first use of the B-1 in an extended campaign. The 'Bone' proved to be the most effective heavy bomber in the Kosovo War, from the standpoint of accuracy, tonnage on target, and reliability. In the conflict's final phases, B-1s were often flown in 'terminal guidance' mode, receiving their target information from the Combined Air Operation Center (CAOC) at Vicenza, Italy when they arrived in the combat area. They were also able to change targets en route without any degradation of accuracy. Nearly 25 years after the first B-1A rolled out, and 15 years after the first B-1B flew, the 'Bone' arrived as one of the most effective long-range bombers ever to go to war.

The B-1's combat history did not end over Kosovo. The worst attack on US soil since World War Two resulted in the 'Bone' returning to action in the skies over Afghanistan.

This Bomb Damage Assessment (BDA) photograph was taken of Ponkive Air Field, Serbia after it was attacked by two B-1s during ALLIED FORCE. Craters from 500 pound bombs litter the airfield area, including the runway and taxiways. Major Serb targets were typically attacked by two B-1s, which dropped up to one hundred sixty eight 500 pound bombs. (via Jeff Warmka)

A reconnaissance image was taken of the Novi Sad petroleum refinery in Yugoslavia, prior to the B-1B raid on 1 May 1999. The facility was slightly damaged in a previous NATO air attack. The refinery is located beside the Danube River in the northern Yugoslav province of Vojvodina. (via Jeff Warmka)

Flames erupt from the Novi Sad refinery after two 77th BS B-1Bs attacked it on the evening of 1 May. The 'Bones' dropped one hundred sixty eight 500 pound bombs on the facility, causing extensive damage. The refinery was a major oil producer for the Serbian armed forces. Both Lancers returned safely to Fairford after the raid. (via Jeff Warmka)

Flying the 'Bone'

"You realize, of course, that this was an even trade." I was being facetious, as I helped Major Scott Cameron unstrap and climb out of my **T-34 Mentor**. We were both performing in the first annual Las Vegas air show in 2000, me with the Lima Lima Flight Team, and Scott as a B-1 demonstration pilot. Our team leader had offered the B-1 crewmembers a demo ride prior to the regular air show and Scott was one of the takers.

Scott looked thoughtful for a moment before saying, *"Well, you know, we might be able to get you a 'Bone' ride."* My research for the B-1 in Action had languished for several years, but this comment sent it immediately to the front burner. It took several months of diligent lobbying on the part of Scott, but the Air Force finally officially approved an orientation ride for me.

Scott 'Fabio' Cameron is a 1988 graduate of the USAF Academy. After a stint of B-52 flying (do all B-1 crew members come from the B-52 community?), Scott was eventually assigned to the B-1. At the time of our flight, he was Chief of Standards and Evaluation for the 7th Operations Group (OG) at Dyess AFB, near Abilene, Texas. The 7th owns the majority of operational B-1s and oversees the training of B-1 initiates by the 28th Bomb Squadron (BS). The 7th also 'owns' the 13th BS and the 9th BS.

When it became pretty certain that this flight was going to happen, I started to wonder just exactly where I would sit during the flight. The B-1 has four crewmembers, but only the pilots have any kind of an outside view. The 'Whizzos' (Offensive Systems Officer, or OSO, and Defensive Systems Officer, or DSO) sit behind the pilots, in darkened, dedicated workspaces. They do have (really) small windows, but the blinds are usually pulled to enhance viewing of the electronic displays. The 'Whizzos' are committed to the formidable job of managing the complex electronics of the 'Bone.' 'Whizzo' is a generic term, a derivation of Weapons Systems Officer (WSO), which was first applied to **F-4 Phantom** backseaters. The B-1 backseaters are cross-trained as OSOs and DSOs, but usually refer to themselves as 'Whizzos.'

Although I really wanted the ride, I was not enthusiastic about sitting in the back. (I confess that I am not a quick study when it comes to complicated electronics, so several hours of trying to understand the B-1's aft cockpit displays seemed like a recipe for a headache.) Nor was I particularly anxious to sit on the foldout jump seat, whose occupant would have to strap on the spare parachute and try to exit through the entry hatch in the bottom of the aircraft in the event of an emergency in-flight departure. I didn't have to worry about the latter. After the first B-1 accident [the crash of 84-0052 on 28 September 1987], in which the occupants of these seats did not get out of the aircraft, the Air Force has mandated that everyone who flies in the B-1 must be in an ejection seat.

"Oh, you'll sit in the left seat" was the most welcome (and surprising) answer to that question. Scott said: *"I'll fly the airplane from the right seat, where I do most of my flying as an instructor anyway. The placement of the gear lever and flaps switch is more convenient for operation by the Co-Pilot anyway. Unfortunately, you can't touch the stick."* (This was in the immediate aftermath of the collision of the submarine USS GREENEVILLE [SSN-772] and a Japanese fishing boat [off Hawaii in 2000]. The media touted the presence of civilians on the GREENEVILLE as a causal factor in the accident and the services were being most careful about civilian control of military hardware.) Much as I would like to have been able to say I flew the B-1, it really seemed more important to watch someone who knew what they were doing flying the jet. 'Jet' has become the generic term for an aircraft throughout the military. Scott even referred to my prop-driven T-34 as a 'Jet.' Although I did not touch the stick while we were airborne, I got my 15 minutes of glory by performing a takeoff and landing in the simulator. (Without crashing!)

Before I could fly, I had to fill some 'get ready' squares the day before the flight. A fast and furious day began at 0730 hours at the front gate, where I received my base pass. From there, it was on to the 28th Bomb Squadron, where we would plan and brief the following day's mission. The 28th is the B-1B Flight Training Unit (FTU), where all aspiring B-1B crew members are trained. Typical classes are approximately ten students each for crew positions (Pilot, Co-Pilot, Offensive Systems Officer, and Defensive Systems Officer). While the OSO and DSO

Two 7th Wing 'Bones' fly a training mission over the western United States. Average B-1B training missions are six hours long and consist of high and low altitude practice bombing, tactical formations, and aerial refueling. The lead aircraft has the blue and white checkerboard tail band of the 28th BS, 7th BW at Dyess AFB, Texas. Both B-1Bs have their wings swept at an intermediate setting for high speed cruising.

positions involve diverse disciplines, they are currently cross-trained, making that curriculum a most intense course. Not that the pilots have an easy time of it. The B-1B is known as one of the most complex aircraft ever built and the pilots are also the engineers, required to have an intimate knowledge of the multiple 'Bone' systems. The 28th averages 40 graduates per year in both Pilot and OSO/DSO positions.

We began our briefing in the large amphitheater. The crews from both aircraft were present, but I only got to sit in on the introduction and weather brief. When they got to the threat briefing, I lacked the necessary secret clearance to keep my seat. (If I had had a clearance, I wouldn't have stayed…what's the point of a writer listening to stuff he can't write about?)

Our mission was laid on for the following day. It was a two ship flight, with two main objectives: An orientation ride for me, and the annual check ride for Lt Col Davis Wallette. Lt Col Wallette conducted the joint briefing, which began with a general overview of the mission. It would include aerial refueling and a combination of high and low simulated attacks. Our OSO, Major Doug 'Caveman' Howard, was assigned the task of picking targets and preparing the target cards. Scott and I were cleared off to take care of the other things necessary for my flight. Our first visit was to the flight surgeon, who examined me and pronounced me fit for flight. The next stop was life support, where I was fitted with a survival vest, torso harness, helmet, and oxygen mask. Then it was on to 7th OG headquarters, where I was introduced to Col Chris Miller, the Commanding Officer (CO). I would be flying in one of his aircraft and he was the guy who had ultimate approval for my flight. After a half-hour of pleasantries and geopolitical discussion, it was time for lunch…at a great local barbecue (BBQ) place. (Do they have any bad BBQ joints in Abilene? I DON'T think so!)

After lunch, I spent an hour with Captain Matt Weller, the 7th OG's egress trainer. The primary egress method (aside from the preferred climbing down the ladder after landing) is the ACES II ejection seat. ACES stands for Advanced Concept Ejection Seat. It was designed and built by McDonnell Douglas Corporation (when there was a McDonnell Douglas Corporation; now, it's Boeing). It is designed to operate in three separate modes. One mode is Low Speed, Low Altitude, defined as below 250 knots (287.9 MPH/463.3 KMH) and below 15,000 feet (4572 M). This is the envelope that provides 'zero-zero' capability. (Zero airspeed, zero altitude.) In this mode, the main parachute deploys as soon as the seat clears the cockpit, inflating within 1.5 seconds. In the moderate speed mode (250-650 knots, below 15,000 feet), the drogue parachute deploys as the seat leaves the cockpit to stabilize the seat, followed by main chute deployment within 2.5 seconds. In the high speed and high altitude mode (250 to 650 knots, above 15,000 feet), the drogue chute deploys as the seat leaves, but deployment of the main chute is delayed until the seat/pilot combination has descended below 15,000 feet. The drogue parachute slows and stabilizes the seat as it descends to the thicker air at low altitude. If the parachute were deployed at high altitude, the seat occupant would be in for a long, cold ride (read hypothermia) to terra firma, and could conceivably run out of emergency oxygen before he got to the ground. Another danger of high altitude deployment in thin air is higher deployment speeds and the possibility of damaging the parachute canopy as a result.

The 'Auto' ejection mode ejects the OSO, DSO, Co-Pilot, and Pilot, in that order. Either of the pilots can initiate this sequence. Automatic separation of the crew after they eject is provided by vectoring of the seat rocket motors. This mode is used in low altitude and/or low speed situations. At mid-to-high altitudes, the ejection mode panel is set to 'MAN' for manual, allowing the crew to determine the order of ejection. I was instructed on how to attach myself to the seat and to the airplane. This was much easier in the seat mockup than it was in the aircraft!

Our last stop in a fairly frenetic day was the simulator (sim). Since I was going to occupy the pilot's seat, Scott wanted to get me as familiar as possible with the few switches I was going to be required to operate. A bonus was the chance to make one takeoff and landing. We had a real short period in the sim, due to Air Force regulations that dictated 12 hours of crew rest before beginning the duty flying day. This meant we had to be out of the sim by 1745 local time.

Even though the simulator provides a visual representation of the outside world through the windshield, you are essentially on instruments, since any tactile sensory inputs provided by the full motion simulator are likely to be foreign to someone who has not been in the aircraft. Trying to make sense of the visuals is likely to induce vertigo. (It got me on taxiing to the active runway!) I did manage to make the takeoff with coaching from Scott, then flew a long pattern to a successful (although scary) landing. The simulator gave me an appreciation for the responsive controls of the 'Bone'…it is almost fighter-like.

Scott had planned a fairly typical, although complex, six hour mission. After takeoff, we would strike a target from high altitude, get into a refueling track with three other 'Bones,' take many air-to-air pictures, then drop into a low level route for some great sight-seeing en route to our second target. Our takeoff time of 0810 dictated a 'step[1]' time of 0600, which worked backwards to an 0430 wakeup. Our call sign was *Hawk* Flight, with dead-meat-me in the left seat, Major Scott 'Fabio' Cameron in the right seat, Major Doug 'Caveman' Howard as OSO, and our second pilot, Captain Jeff 'Flash' Warmka occupying the DSO seat. We were *Hawk 74. Hawk 73* would lead the two-ship flight, with Lt Col Davis 'Wally' Wallette flying, Lt Col Rob Gass in the right seat, Captain Bob Loy and Major Jon Schilder in the back. This was an annual check ride for 'Wally,' so he was anxious to get the mission flown.

[1]Step time was the time aircrewmen stepped out of the briefing room and onto the crew bus for transport to the aircraft.

A B-1B flies with its wings at the minimum sweep angle of 15°. The B-1's broad, flat underside acts as a lifting body, enhancing the performance of the bomber. The three internal weapons bays have a load carrying capacity of 75,000 pounds (34,020 KG), exceeding the B-52's 54,000 pound (24,494.4 KG) internal load capacity. (Lt Col Tracy Sharp)

Major Scott Cameron checks the starboard main landing gear on his pre-flight walk around the B-1B while the crew chief pulls the safety pins from the gear. The crew chief stands on the A-frame side brace connecting the forward gear well bulkhead to the main strut. Landing gear assemblies and wheel wells are Gloss White (FS17875) to easily detect liquid leaks. The robust gear fully retracts under hydraulic power in 40 seconds. (Lou Drendel)

It was a dark and stormy night when I awoke. Well, it was dark and wet anyway. There was a 700 foot (213.4 M) ceiling and two mile (3.2 KM) visibility with light rain. Since the temperature was above 35° Fahrenheit (1.7° Celsius), we were saved from the icing restriction. (B-1s do have anti-ice on the engine 'bullet nose' and on the inlet vane, but not on the Radar Cross Section [RCS] baffle. Temperatures between 20 and 35° F [-6.7° and 1.7° C] can cause icing on this vane and create the potential for Foreign Object Damage [FOD] to the engines. Engines are currently being upgraded to cure these problems. Since the F101 engines cost in the neighborhood of $6 million each, this is no small consideration.) The squadron operations center started to fill up after 0530. Besides our two crews, the crews of *Tex 1* and *Tex 2* were hanging out. They were scheduled for takeoff shortly after us, and we were hoping to join up with them in the Air Refueling (AR) track.

We got our first bad news of the day when we were informed that *Hawk 73* would not be going anywhere until they located a missing screwdriver. The 'Bone' is a large, complicated aircraft. Maintenance is an around-the-clock affair and the current crew had discovered that a tool was missing from the previous shift. Since this tool had the potential to create a major catastrophe, the aircraft would not move until it was found. We debated taking off without them, then meeting them later in the AR track, but ultimately decided to push the flight for a couple of hours. This gave us a chance to re-brief the whole deal.

We finally stepped onto the crew bus at 0815. First stop was the 28th BS Life Support unit, where I picked up my helmet, mask, survival vest, and torso harness. All of these items had been painstakingly fitted the day before by Sgt Pena and his capable crew. (No small feat. This stuff is not designed for comfort, so when they ask you how it feels, telling the truth does not necessarily elicit pity or remedial action.)

'Flash' (Warmka) and 'Caveman' (Howard) began loading our equipment aboard SPECTRE (86-0109), a Block D 'Bone' of the 28th BS, as soon as we got off the bus. Scott did the walk around, with me following. This inspection is designed to let another pair of experienced eyes look for any obvious anomalies. Scott paid particular attention to the tires, which take a beating and have the potential to create big problems if they blow during takeoff.

The cockpit preflight is a long and detailed procedure. 'Fabio' had asked 'Flash' to sit in the left seat during this procedure to speed things up and make sure they were done right. While they were going through their checklists, 'Caveman' was aligning the Inertial Navigation Systems (INS), giving the Global Positioning System (GPS) time to acquire, and adjusting the various antennas. During all of this, there were several electrical glitches. The crew referred to these as 'EMUX issues.' EMUX stands for Electrical Multiplex system, which as you might guess is a controller for several of the electrical boxes. EMUX was a revolutionary addition to the B-1. It eliminated over 29,000 wires and 80 miles (128.7 KM) of wiring from major electrical subsystems and was likened by Rockwell to the human spinal column. EMUX performs the functions of data conditioning, acquisition, command, and control for over 9000 inputs and signals. It is one of the features of the B-1 that makes it the most complex aircraft ever built. The crew members jokingly refer to EMUX as 'HAL.' (HAL was the computer who developed a malevolent and somewhat inscrutable personality in the movie "2001, A Space Odyssey.") While these EMUX issues weren't immediately mission threatening, they did call for specialists to come to the cockpit to check 'switchology' (how the switches work) and trouble-shoot the symptoms. When they finally got things set, they ushered me into the left seat.

There are nine separate connections between you and the aircraft. Some are easy, but most are fairly tough when you are doing it for the first time. (I got better after the third repetition.) Two connections hold you to the seat, there are two connections to the parachute risers, a lap belt, leg restraints, oxygen hose, communications (com) cord, and the CRU-60 connector holding the oxygen and com leads in place on your torso harness. The survival vest, with its pouches full of the necessities for survival in the wilds of wherever, makes it tough to see what you are doing until you perfect your technique.

I finally got settled in and was ready to go when there was another electrical hiccup. The crew chief suggested that we shut down the generators and then power them up again to fool the computers into thinking it was a whole new day. That seemed to do the trick and we were cleared to taxi. The pilots like to joke that there is no single individual at any unit that knows everything about the B-1 systems. There is only one 'Super Engineer,' buried deep in the bowels of Boeing, that knows it all. This is probably not far from the truth, although the 'Super Engineer' is no doubt a composite of many Boeing engineers.

It takes a pretty good shot of power to get the 'Bone' rolling. We left the chocks at a gross weight of 360,000 pounds (163,296 KG), which included over 150,000 pounds (68,040 KG) of fuel distributed throughout the fuselage and wings. The 'Bone' can carry up to 204,000 pounds (92,534.4 KG) of fuel. One of the most important tasks of its automated systems is management of the ever-decreasing fuel load to maintain Center of Gravity (CG) within limits. This is complicated by the shifting CG caused by swinging the wings through the 15° full forward position to the 67.5° full aft position. That is not the only complex aspect of the fuels system. Fuel is also used as a heat sink to cool the B-1's myriad black boxes, so it follows a serpentine route to the engines. Soon after we began rolling forward, Scott applied the brakes to make sure they were working, then turned right to head for the active runway.

Dyess has some of the roughest concrete I have ever experienced, both on taxiways and runways, so it was not a particularly smooth ride to the end of the active runway. Our wingman, in a 'Bone' from the 13th BS 'Reapers,' followed us to the run-up pad, where we did the final checks, snapped our masks into place, lowered our face shields and called the control tower for takeoff clearance. *"Hawk 74, fly runway heading, maintain 4000* [feet/1219.2 M]*, cleared for takeoff."* Scott repeated the clearance and taxied into position on runway 16.

With the nose lined up on the centerline, he smoothly applied power with the brakes set. Engine instruments showed normal at mil (military[2]) power, so he bumped the throttles to min(inum) afterburner. Still normal, so he went to full blower [afterburner] and after a quick glance to confirm full power on all engines, he released the brakes and we were rolling. The F101 engine develops 32,000 pounds of thrust in full afterburner, so acceleration is brisk, although not fighter-like.

"Hawk 74, Abort! Abort! Abort!" Our wingman had heard three distinct 'whumps,' (we felt nothing) and saw flames shooting out of our number three (right inboard) engine. Scott quickly retarded the throttles and announced that he was aborting the takeoff on the runway. The tower announced that they had seen flames coming from the left side of the aircraft, which meant engines one or two. They also rolled two fire trucks, an ambulance, and several associated maintenance vehicles. *Hawk 73* announced that he was also aborting and would follow us back to parking. En route to parking, Wallette volunteered to give us his jet so I could get my ride. When we cleared the runway, the maintenance chief made a quick visual inspection of the rear of the aircraft and announced that there was some damage to the number three engine nozzle. (They also found pieces of metal on the runway.) It was later discovered that defective roller bearings had disintegrated, damaging the burner section of the number three engine.

Hawk 73 was parked a short distance away, with the engines running. The crew bus shuttled

[2]Military Power: The maximum non-afterburning power setting on an engine.

SPECTRE is a B-1B (86-0109) assigned to the 28th Bomb Squadron, 7th Bomb Wing at Dyess AFB. The Squadron insignia is placed aft of the nose art. This Lancer was designated *Hawk 74* for the author's orientation flight from Dyess on 28 March 2001. Engine problems on takeoff forced an abort and a subsequent change to a different B-1 (*Hawk 73*) for the author's flight. (Lou Drendel)

The 'crew' of *Hawk 74* pose before their 'Bone' (left to right): The author, Maj Scott Cameron, Maj Doug Howard, and Lt Col Jeff Warmka. Howard was the only Weapons System Officer (WSO) on this flight. Warmka is a combat veteran B-1B pilot, having flown 17 missions during Operation ALLIED FORCE in 1999. (Davis Wallette)

The author sits in the port (Pilot's) seat...hands off the controls. The strap over the shoulder pulls the arms in on ejection, preventing flailing injuries. The ACES II seats fitted to the B-1B incorporate an added cushion on the seat back and bottom for a more comfortable ride on long flights. (Maj Scott Cameron)

us to our new jet and as the crew of *Hawk 73* exited, we replaced them. While we taxied past *Hawk 74*, I noted that the crew chief was in the starboard intake and the crew had already opened up the nacelle in preparation for replacing the number three engine. The ground crewmen are usually in their twenties and this young chief was no exception. The Air Force had given him the responsibility for the maintenance of a $280 million aircraft and he and his crew were taking it most seriously.

The B-1's complexities never seem to end and neither do the checks – preflight, in-flight, post-flight – they are seemingly interminable. We had to make a 90° left turn, followed by a 90° right turn on our way to the active. As we swung to the right, Scott let me know he was checking the operation of the turn and bank indicator. Yes, even the most complicated collection of airborne electronics still obeys the basic laws of aerodynamics and uses the venerable needle and ball to verify coordinated flight. Ninety degree turns should result in full deflection of the needle one way and the ball the other way. (It did.)

Although we had changed aircraft [to 86-0105], we wanted to re-file our *Hawk 74* flight plan, although we were now flying *Hawk 73*. This caused some confusion in the Air Traffic Control (ATC) ranks and we waited them out at the run-up pad. When the clearance came through, it was the same as our original takeoff instruction. This time the acceleration was smooth and uneventful. At 161 knots (185.4 MPH/298.4 KMH), Scott raised the nose 8° and the big bomber came unstuck and began to climb. Scott was busy, flipping the gear lever up, and retracting the flaps and slats, as we climbed at 360 knots (414.5 MPH/667.1 KMH), with the wings swept at 25°.

Departure gave us a right turn, direct to Panhandle VHF Omnidirectional Radio (VOR), near Amarillo, Texas. This was our Initial Point (IP) for the first bomb run. In the climb, Scott conferred with 'Caveman' about the possibility of finding a tanker. We had lost our scheduled tanker with the delay in the original flight plan. In fact, our original flight plan had been truncated and we were now anticipating a four hour sortie. Aerial refueling was problematic, unless we could find a spare tanker. Scott asked 'Caveman' to get on the tanker common frequency and see if he could make a deal. This was literally what happened. *Wiley* Flight was a pair of Kansas Air National Guard (ANG) **KC-135**s [117th Air Refueling Squadron, 190th Air Refueling Group from Forbes Field]. They were about at the end of their fuel and coming up on a turn for Topeka.

Complicating this was our altitude restriction of 18,000 feet (5486.4 M), imposed because I did not have a current altitude chamber training card.[3] (Tanker refueling tracks are typically flown in the low 20s.) It took some salesmanship (including the fact that I was doing a book and would make them famous) to get *Wiley 32* to agree to drag us toward Topeka. When we told ATC what we wanted to do, they let us know that they could not agree to AR below 18,000 feet. (FL[Flight Level]-180 is the threshold of positive control. Anything below that is available to Visual Flight Rules [VFR] aircraft.) Our only hope was to accomplish the AR in a Military Operating Area (MOA), which gave us some protection from VFR traffic. Scott and 'Caveman' were able to convince the 'Kansas Coyotes' (117th ARS tankers) to stretch their

[3]All aircrew members, from all services, are required to attend refresher training periodically. This includes a session in the altitude chamber to demonstrate the effects of hypoxia (a blood deficiency caused by a lack of oxygen). USAF regulations restrict flight to below 18,000 feet (5486.4 M) if you are not 'chamber current.' I had not attended one of these classes in over ten years and was not considered current.

The 'Bone' in which the author eventually flew his orientation flight was 86-0105, call sign *Hawk 73*. It was assigned to the 13th Bomb Squadron, 'The Devil's Own Grim Reapers,' 7th Bomb Wing. Overall finish is Dark Gunship Gray (FS36081) with a red tail band displaying REAPERS in white. (Lou Drendel)

sortie to accommodate our AR. Up to this point, we had been VFR on top of a solid undercast. In fact, we had spotted one of their tankers dragging a **C-5** to the southeast as we were northbound. Naturally, as soon as we got agreement on the AR mission, we were in and out of the 'clag' [slang term for Instrument Flight Rules (IFR) conditions]. 'Caveman' had the tanker on radar and we made a smooth rendezvous as the tanker began flying a triangular track in the MOA.

Aerial refueling is one of the most demanding duties that military pilots perform. It is not just flying formation. It is flying formation on a winged pole that is waving in the turbulent wake of a hundreds of thousands of pounds of flying gas station. I had my shot at this in the B-1 simulator at Ellsworth AFB, along with the rest of the Lima Lima Flight Team. We consider ourselves to be pretty good formation pilots, but none of us could manage a successful hook up. The B-1 refueling door is immediately in front of the pilots, on the top of the nose, so you get a really good look at the boom as you fly up to it and give the boomer in the tanker a shot at plugging in. Once you are connected, it is the responsibility of the receiver to maintain good position and stay plugged.

As we approached the tanker, we entered solid instrument conditions. Visibility was pretty good in the clouds, but there was no horizon to provide positional clues. Scott was very smooth as he drove up to the boom and let the boomer [boom operator] in the KC-135 stab us in the nose. Once connected, I was impressed by the increased noise level and the turbulence. I'm not sure how much of the latter was caused by the weather, but it was a factor in maintaining position. I glanced over at Scott to check out his technique, and was amazed to see him holding the stick delicately between his thumb and forefinger. His left hand was moving the four throttles in increments of fractions of an inch as he toe-danced the 150 ton (136.1 MT) bomber along behind the tanker.

After two circuits around the AR track, we dropped off and headed west for our entry to the low-level portion of our mission. The B-1 was designed to attack targets deep in enemy territory and the mandate for the designers was low-level, high-speed, all-weather penetration to avoid the threat of Surface-to-Air Missiles (SAMs). The mission has since changed with the enhancement of defenses to defeat SAMs. Now the primary threat is from Anti-Aircraft Artillery (AAA), which can be dangerous even when it is not directed by radar. Most of the combat losses to anti-aircraft fire during and since Vietnam have been to AAA, so it is now considered prudent to drop bombs from altitudes beyond AAA range, which generally means in the mid-20,000 foot regime. (All of the combat missions flown by the B-1 have employed this profile.) That does not mean that the USAF will never use the low level capability of the B-1, so the crews still practice in the dirt. The pilots like this because it is the best kind of flying. I am not so sure the guys in the back are that crazy about being bounced around by low level turbulence and the frequent turns, or violent ups and downs of hard ride terrain following.

We crossed the Continental Divide at 17,000 feet (5181.6 M), then began a slow descent through mixed layers of clouds, with glimpses of snow-covered mountains sliding by below. We broke into the clear before our entry into the low level route. With the autopilot flying, we leveled off at 1000 feet (304.8 M) above the ground. The Terrain Following Radar (TFR) was set on 'Hard Ride.' (There are three TFR modes: Hard, Medium, and Soft. Hard Ride gives

The author flies at 540 knots (621.8 MPH/1000.7 KMH), below the canyon rim! The B-1B flew through Bryce Canyon in southern Utah at approximately 500 feet (152.4 M) Above Ground Level (AGL). The 'Bone' is known as the bomber that flies like a fighter and the low level portion of this flight proved the agility of the big bomber during Scott Cameron's demonstration of a modified nap of the earth technique. (Lou Drendel)

The aerial refueling boom of a Kansas ANG KC-135E (call sign *Wiley 32*) prepares to plug into *Hawk 74*'s receptacle. Insertion of the refueling boom into the receptacle shuts off all transfer pumps, opens the Ballast Tank Isolation Valve, and opens all fill valves. As each tank fills, the fill valves shut off flow into the tank. Careful Center of Gravity (CG) management is critical during refueling to prevent losing aircraft control. (Lou Drendel)

Major Scott 'Fabio' Cameron flew the author's orientation flight from the co-pilot seat. He has one hand on the throttles while he checks off flight benchmarks prior to crossing the Continental Divide. The benchmarks are placed on a kneeboard strapped to Cameron's left leg for easy in-flight access. (Lou Drendel)

you up to 2.5 G (2.5 times the force of gravity) pull-ups and less than that for push-overs to follow the terrain profile, which is shown graphically on the pilot's display. The ground is represented by a series of jagged lines...just what you would expect from radar returns...while the aircraft's flight path is shown as a solid line.)

Although the autopilot was flying the profile, Scott was controlling the throttles. (Auto throttle is also available to maintain a constant airspeed throughout the TFR profile.) 'Caveman' was busily updating us on our course data, including what we could expect to see out of the windshield. There is a 1000 foot limit on use of the TFR, but pilots are allowed to hand-fly the aircraft down to 500 feet (152.4 M), so after I was suitably impressed with the capabilities of the automatic system, Scott took over and descended for our final approach to the target.

The target was listed as a road intersection, heavily populated by enemy troops. We would be simulating the dropping of fifty-six 500 pound (226.8 KG) Mk 82 bombs to depopulate the intersection. The target card that 'Caveman' had prepared was a comprehensive picture of the target area, which also showed the sun azimuth (horizontal bearing) and angle, (Azimuth 130, Elevation 46°) and the lethal cone of bomb fragments (2600 feet [792.5 M] Horizontal, 2225 feet [678.2 M] Vertical). One of the dangers of low-level bombing is the possibility of 'fragging' yourself if you are unable to clear the impact area quickly enough. Although you generally think of this part of the United States as being pretty much devoid of civilization, there was still traffic on the highways and small, hardscrabble rancheros that we blasted over at 600+ MPH (965.6+ KMH). It has got to be impressive to see the big, dark gray bomber streaking by overhead with the wings swept at 67.5°! It is a fearsome sight with the bomb bay doors open, which is why they are not opened for simulated drops. I looked down at the target card and the associated strip map to check for landmarks. There are few of them in this part of the country...at least not the kind you are used to seeing. The radar picture was slightly more distinctive and there were cross checks as we made our target run. At 16 miles (25.7 KM), 'Caveman' cross checked point 18-1 at 45° left angle off of our 284° run in course, 15 nautical miles (17.3 miles/27.8 KM) away. We picked up the little cluster of buildings around the target when we were still ten miles (16.1 KM) out, but at our speed, that equated to less than a minute. At two miles (3.2 KM), he cross-checked point 18-2 at 45° angle off to the right at 23 miles (37 KM). The navigation was precise and at less than one mile (1.6 KM), the doors were called open and bombs came out as we blasted over the center of the intersection at 600 feet (182.9 M) above ground. (I wondered if there was some skin crawling on those folks down there...did they know they had just been pulverized?)

Once we were off the target, it was time for some serious evasive, low-level flying. Just in time too, since we were entering the Bryce Canyon area of southern Utah. This is marked by some of the most spectacular scenery you will ever see and believe me, it is more impressive at 500 feet (152.4 M) Above Ground Level (AGL)! Scott flew a strict terrain avoidance schedule, trying to maintain a relatively constant Mean Sea Level (MSL[4]) altitude, which meant a lot of flying through cuts and canyons. In consideration to the guys in the back, he called every turn that was made as he rolled left and right. Since the 'Whizzos' usually have their heads buried in their scopes, they like to keep the shades pulled on the small windows next to their seats. Aggressive maneuvering at low altitude is a sure recipe for nausea if you are prone to vertigo and losing your outside reference. The turn calls helped the 'Whizzos' to relate their seat of the pants feelings as the big bomber rode through the low-level turbulence of late afternoon.

[4]Mean Sea Level: The average sea surface height, usually calculated from hourly tide readings measured over a 19 year period.

A B-1B (86-0137) assigned to the 13th Bomb Squadron 'Reapers' from Dyess AFB seeks in-flight refueling. The wings are swept at 25° for this cruise to the tanker rendezvous. The pilot or co-pilot may select any sweep angle between 15° and 67.5°, depending upon flight conditions. (Lt Col Tracy Sharp)

Every military aircraft I have ever flown in has some characteristic that remained with me long after the flight. My first ride in an F-4 produced amazement at the stiff legged, jarring taxi. The F-16 is memorable for its comfort level because of the reclining seat. The F-18 was one of the more uncomfortable aircraft. The seat felt like a rock and Gs coming off target seemed interminable. The power of the F-15 was unforgettable. The **A-1** was oily and noisy. The B-52 takeoff – when the water injection ran out – was scary. The Mach One plus low level speed of the **F-111** left rooster tails behind us in the desert. The smooth and honest controls of the T-34 seduced me on the first flight, starting a 27 year love affair.

The 'Bone' is memorable for the noises, both quantity and quality. The big vanes on the nose, which help to maintain stability, are in constant motion (they are computer-controlled) and produce highly pronounced 'thunk-clunk' noises as they cycle. They are the most visible feature of the Low Altitude Ride Control (LARC) system. [LARC is also called the Structural Mode Control System, SMCS.] The vanes are derived from the 'exciter vanes' mounted on the Rockwell-built triplesonic XB-70 research aircraft. There are plenty of other noises from the back of the aircraft. They are hard to describe, but are most disconcerting to a pilot who is only used to associating noises like that with bad things. Most of these noises were caused by airframe flexing, which is normal, but is accentuated from the crew's standpoint because of the cockpit's extreme forward location. Without LARC, which suppresses bending in all directions, the flexing would be much more severe. The ride is hard, but watching Scott fly the aircraft left me with the distinct impression that this 150 ton bomber was flying like a much smaller and lighter fighter.

Those are the basic impressions. The more important, and relevant, impressions have to do with the way a competent crew can think on the fly and make things happen. It is how they are able to operate in the most complex and demanding mission environment of the 'Bone.' There are only 75 out of 95 B-1s available for duty at any given time. (Funding restrictions keep the others on the ground.) Given the worldwide mission of power projection they are required to perform and the effectiveness with which they have done this mission, you have to feel that your tax dollars are being well spent. To borrow an in-vogue advertising slogan, "These Guys Are Good!"

The crew of *Hawk 73*, whose mission was postponed and ultimately flown in NIGHT Stalker (86-0117) included (left to right): Lt Col Rob Gass, Lt Col Davis Wallette, Maj Jon Schilder, and Capt Bob Loy. Nose art is painted in full colors, while unit insignia are in subdued colors. The 28th BS emblem appears aft of the NIGHT Stalker art and below the Defensive Systems Officer's window. (Lou Drendel)

Operation ENDURING FREEDOM

While this book goes to press, Operation ENDURING FREEDOM – the campaign against international terrorism – is just a few months into what President Bush promised would be a long, hard conflict. If truth is the first casualty of war, then timely reporting is surely in the front ranks of casualties. Fortunately, modern communications goes a long way towards mitigating the fog of war. Pictures are invariably the most reliable records of current campaigns. You can believe most of what you see, if not much of what you read. With that in mind, we are presenting some of the first photos of B-1 operations in the current war, with limited editorial comment.

The year 2001 saw further constrictions in the B-1 force, as additional bombers were 'defunded' and added to the ranks of temporarily-parked-and-used-as-spare-parts-inventory. (In order to keep all of the B-1s viable, aircraft are rotated through this pool. The funding keeps a percentage of the total force flying operational missions.)

B-1s have played a central role in the strikes against Afghanistan. Following the 11 September 2001 terrorist attacks on the World Trade Center in New York City and the Pentagon in Washington, President George W. Bush ordered attacks on Afghanistan's Taliban government and on the terrorist networks it sponsored. Attacks were particularly ordered on the facilities of al-Qaeda, the terrorist organization run by Saudi-born Osama bin Laden.

Under the operational command of the 28th Air Expeditionary Wing (AEW), B-1Bs are flying missions against Afghanistan from the Indian Ocean island of Diego Garcia. Diego Garcia is a 17 square mile (44 KM²) coral atoll in the central Indian Ocean. It is in the Chagos

An ordnance specialist prepares 2000 pound (907.2 KG) Joint Direct Attack Munitions (JDAMs) for loading aboard a 77th Bomb Squadron B-1B at Diego Garcia. JDAMs are modified Mark 80 series 'iron' bombs fitted with centerbody strakes, which provide aerodynamic lift to the weapon. Tail-mounted Global Positioning System (GPS) receivers ensure precise JDAM delivery to the target. (USAF)

An Air Force bomb loader driving an MJ-1 lift truck delivers a 2000 pound JDAM to a B-1B prior to a mission over Afghanistan. Towed Decoy System (TDS) fairings are mounted on the port and starboard tail cone sides. Expendable countermeasures housed in the TDS fairings help protect the Lancer from Surface-to-Air Missiles (SAMs) – a threat which did not materialize during these missions. (USAF)

A B-1B takes off from Diego Garcia for Afghanistan on 7 October 2001. The Lancer attacked Taliban and al-Qaeda targets during Operation ENDURING FREEDOM – the US response to the terrorist attacks of 11 September 2001. Five other 'Bones' are parked on the ramp, across from a KC-10 tanker/transport. (USAF)

Archipelago, which is part of the British Indian Ocean Territory. Since the late 1970s, the US has used Diego Garcia as a base for operations in southwest and south Asia. Living conditions for flight crews and ground personnel on the island are spartan. The USAF ground crews worked around the clock in the first three weeks of the campaign, before settling into a routine of 12-hour shifts.

Lancers assigned to the 28th AEW are drawn from the 28th Bomb Wing (BW) at Ellsworth AFB, South Dakota; the 366th Wing at Mountain Home AFB, Idaho; and the 7th BW at Dyess AFB, Texas. B-1B missions from Diego Garcia are 12 to 15 hours in length and cover total distances up to 5500 miles (8851.2 KM). Bombing missions have been flown against a variety of Taliban and al-Qaeda targets, including early warning radars, ground forces, command-and-control facilities, airfields, and aircraft. More than two thirds of the bombs dropped were Precision Guided Munitions (PGMs), using either laser or Global Positioning System (GPS) guidance to hit their targets.

During the initial phases of the air war against the Taliban and al-Qaeda, US Department of Defense (DOD) sources attributed 80% of the missions to heavy bombers. The bomber force was comprised of B-1B, **B-2A Spirit**, and B-52H Stratofortress aircraft. The B-1s and B-52s deployed from the US to Diego Garcia, from where they flew their missions. All B-2 missions originated at their home airfield, Whiteman AFB in Missouri. After making their attacks, the Spirits recovered at Diego Garcia for a crew rest period before returning to Whiteman.

A KC-10 boom operator ('boomer') refuels a B-1B en route to Afghanistan. The refueling boom is 'flown' by the boom operator to help ensure its proper position during refueling. Lancer missions to Afghanistan cover round trip distances up to 5500 miles (8851.2 KM). These require one refueling on the outbound leg and another on the return to Diego Garcia. (USAF)

A 28th Air Expeditionary Wing (AEW) B-1B on full afterburner departs Diego Garcia for another raid on Afghanistan. Lancers from three US-based Wings – the 7th and 28th BWs and the 366th Wing – are assigned to the 28th AEW for Operation ENDURING FREEDOM. Vapor vortices from flying through the humid tropical air stream from the B-1B's port wingtip. (USAF)

Unexpended 500 pound (226.8 KG) Mk 82 bombs are removed from a B-1B on Diego Garcia after a mission against Taliban targets in Afghanistan. This B-1B, SPECTRE (86-0109), is the aircraft the author was originally to have flown his orientation flight from Dyess AFB, Texas on 28 March 2001. An engine problem aborted this mission and his flight was made in another 'Bone.' (USAF)

Bombs Away!

More US Bombers from squadron/signal publications

1042 B-36 Peacemaker

1063 B-17 Flying Fortress

1080 B-24 Liberator

1130 B-52 Stratofortress

1148 A-3 Skywarrior

1165 B-29 Superfortress

1178 B-2 Spirit

5506 B-52 Walk Around

5516 B-17 Walk Around